Iran

Iran

BY JOANN MILIVOJEVIC

Enchantment of the World™
Second Series

Children's Press®

An Imprint of Scholastic Inc.

NEW YORK TORONTO LONDON AUCKLAND SYDNEY
MEXICO CITY NEW DELHI HONG KONG
DANBURY, CONNECTICUT

Frontispiece: Women in rural Iran walk to a pond to wash clothes.

Consultant: Peter Sluglett, Professor of Middle Eastern History, University of Utah, Salt Lake City

Please note: All statistics are as up-to-date as possible at the time of publication.

Book production by Herman Adler

Library of Congress Cataloging-in-Publication Data

Milivojevic, JoAnn.
  Iran / by JoAnn Milivojevic.
      p. cm.—(Enchantment of the world. Second series)
  Includes bibliographical references and index.
  ISBN-13: 978-0-531-18484-4
  ISBN-10: 0-531-18484-6
  1. Iran. I. Title.
  DS254.5.M55 2008
  955—dc22   2007025794

SCHOLASTIC, CHILDREN'S PRESS, and associated logos are trademarks and/or registered trademarks of Scholastic Inc.
1 2 3 4 5 6 7 8 9 10 R 17 16 15 14 13 12 11 10 09 08

Iran

Contents

Cover photo:
Azadi Tower

Isfahan

Iranian girl

CHAPTER ONE

Tradition and Change

8

IN 1979, IRAN BECAME THE WORLD'S FIRST ISLAMIC REPUBLIC. One of the many new laws enacted then required women to cover their hair and wear a loose garment concealing the shape of their body in public. According to the conservative Muslim religious leaders who rule the country, this is the proper modest dress for Muslim women. Interestingly, more than forty years earlier, when Reza Shah Pahlavi was in power, women were forbidden to wear the traditional robes that covered them from head to toe. Missing from both laws is a woman's right to choose how she wants to dress. Buffeted by political changes, Iranian women have not stood idly by. Their voices and their protests form the backbone of the country's fight for human rights.

Opposite: **A woman in southern Iran wears a traditional mask called a nakab. In this area, married women generally wear red masks, and unmarried women wear black masks.**

Reza Shah Pahlavi ruled Iran from 1925 until 1941. During his reign, he tried to westernize the country.

Shirin Ebadi's voice has been loud and clear. She is the first Muslim woman and the first Iranian to receive the Nobel Peace Prize. She was given the prize for her work in defense of the rights of women and children and for promoting democracy in Iran.

Ebadi grew up in the capital city of Tehran in the 1950s and 1960s. It was a time of modernization in Iran. Wealthier men and women wore the latest fashions from Europe and dined at French restaurants. Boys and girls played together freely. Most went to schools that admitted both boys and girls. At the same time, Muslim traditions were still very much a part of daily life. Families were close, and people observed the Muslim holidays.

Shirin Ebadi won the Nobel Peace Prize in 2003. She was given the award for her efforts to advance human rights in Iran.

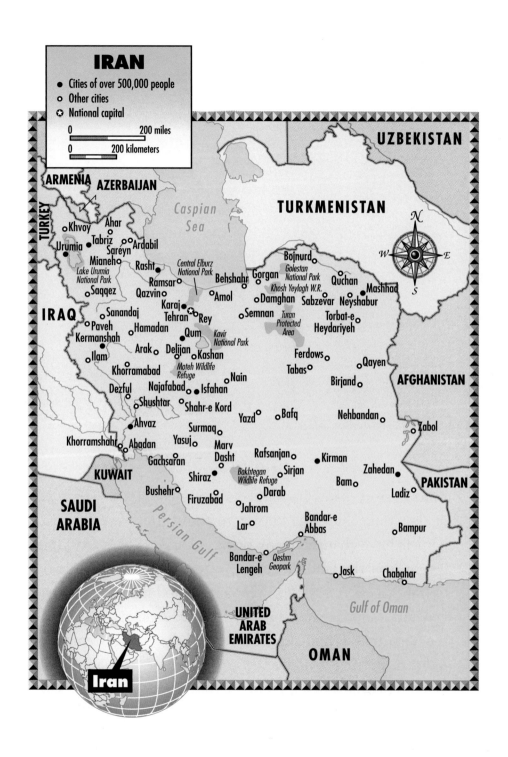

IRAN

- ● Cities of over 500,000 people
- ○ Other cities
- ✪ National capital

0   200 miles

0   200 kilometers

ARMENIA   AZERBAIJAN

UZBEKISTAN

TURKEY

Caspian Sea

TURKMENISTAN

Khvoy   Ahar

Urumia   Tabriz

Sareyn   Ardabil

Mianeh   Rasht

Lake Urumia National Park

Ramsar

Central Elburz National Park

Behshahr   Gorgan

Bojnurd

Golestan National Park

Khosh Yeylagh W.R.

Quchan

Mashhad

Saqqez   Qazvin

Amol

Damghan

Sabzevar   Neyshabur

IRAQ

Sanandaj

Karaj

Tehran   Rey

Semnan

Turan Protected Area

Torbat-e Heydariyeh

Paveh   Hamadan

Kermanshah

Qum

Kavir National Park

Ilam   Arak   Delijan

Kashan

Ferdows

Khorramabad

Moteh Wildlife Refuge

Nain

Tabas

Qayen

Dezful   Najafabad

Isfahan

Birjand

AFGHANISTAN

Shushtar

Shahr-e Kord

Ahvaz

Surmaq

Yazd   Bafq

Nehbandan

Zabol

Khorramshahr   Abadan

Yasuj

Marv Dasht

Rafsanjan

Kirman

Zahedan

PAKISTAN

KUWAIT

Gachsaran

Shiraz

Bakhtegan Wildlife Refuge

Sirjan

Bam

Ladiz

SAUDI ARABIA

Bushehr   Firuzabad

Darab

Bandar-e Abbas

Bampur

Persian Gulf

Jahrom

Lar

Bandar-e Lengeh

Qeshm Geopark

Jask

Chabahar

UNITED ARAB EMIRATES

Gulf of Oman

OMAN

Iran

Under Prime Minister Muhammad Musaddiq (above right), Iran nationalized its oil industry. The United States and Great Britain later helped oust him.

Iran's history dates back several thousand years. For much of that time, Iran was known to the world as Persia. Iran's borders have changed many times as various conquerors have fought over the land. In recent history, the battle for control of Iran has been less for the land itself and more for what lies beneath its surface: oil. In the 1950s, Muhammad Musaddiq, the country's prime minister, nationalized the Iranian oil industry, putting it under the control of the Iranian government. That move made him a national hero, but it upset the United States and Great Britain.

British and American companies were making huge profits from Iran's oil industry. Musaddiq felt they were getting too much. He thought that more of the profits should go to the people of Iran. The Western powers disagreed. Before long, the United States helped overthrow Musaddiq. Mohammad Reza Shah Pahlavi (Reza Shah's son), an unpopular ruler who had briefly fled the country, was brought back to power.

Born in 1947, Shirin Ebadi was just six years old when Musaddiq was removed from office. Her life didn't change much at that time. But as political power continued to change hands, her life would change drastically, and not for the better. In her twenties, she enjoyed the freedom to pursue a law career, and she became Iran's first female judge. But in 1979, when Iran became an Islamic republic, she was fired from her job. Suddenly,

Iran is the fourth-largest oil producer in the world. It pumps nearly four million barrels of oil out of the ground every day.

women were no longer allowed to be judges or hold many other important jobs. Both men and women would lose many other rights and freedoms under the Islamic republic. In her book *Iran Awakening*, Ebadi describes how life changed under the Islamic republic, especially for women.

Ebadi is a devout Muslim and does not believe that religion needs to be a barrier to women's rights. It is the interpretation of the religion that causes problems. Like all religions, Islam has instructions on how to live a proper spiritual life. The question is how these instructions should be applied to daily life. Ebadi argues Iran could reinterpret the laws of Islam to create equality for all its citizens.

Shirin Ebadi is the author of *Iran Awakening*. It tells the story of her career as a lawyer and Iran's first ever female judge.

SHIRIN EBADI

Ein Leben zwischen Revolution und Hoffnung

MEIN IRAN

Die Autobiografie der Friedens-Nobelpreisträgerin

Iran has a thriving film industry. More than one hundred films are produced in the country each year.

Balancing Act

Iran has an ancient history and a rich culture. While today's newspaper headlines about Iran often mention its oil resources, Iran has given the world much more throughout its long history. It had the world's first organized highway and postal systems. Its ancient engineers built underground canals and windmills. Iranian architects inspired the world, and Iranian poets stirred the soul. In recent years, Iran has developed a highly regarded film industry.

It has also, during times of great difficulty, given rise to people like Shirin Ebadi. She and many others like her have shown the world that Iranians will fight for human rights as they struggle to find a balance between traditional religion and the modern world.

CHAPTER

TWO

Mountains and Deserts

I RAN IS FILLED WITH HARSH LANDSCAPES. BARREN MOUN-tains and forbidding deserts sprawl across much of the country, though it also has fertile lowlands. Although most of Iran is arid, not all parts of the country suffer from extreme desert temperatures. In fact, snow falls in Tehran in the winter.

Iran lies in southwestern Asia. It shares borders with seven countries. To the north are Armenia, Azerbaijan, and Turkmenistan, along with the Caspian Sea. To the east are

Opposite: **A man and his donkeys cross the slopes of Mount Damavand, the highest peak in Iran.**

An aerial view of the Persian Gulf coast

Beneath the Ground

Iran has many notable caves. One of the world's longest known salt caves lies beneath the rocky ground on the island of Qeshm in the Persian Gulf. The cave is more than 21,588 feet (6,580 m) long. It has amazing stalactites, which hang from the cave's ceiling like giant fingers.

The 'Alisadr Caves are in western Iran. The caves are partly filled with water, so people tour them by boat. The Ghoori-Ghale Cave, near the Iraqi border, has four waterfalls. It is one of the largest and most impressive water caves in Asia. The water in the Ghoori-Ghale Cave is 10,301 feet (3,140 m) deep.

Afghanistan and Pakistan. Western Iran borders Iraq and Turkey. Most of Iran's southern side skims along the Persian Gulf and the Gulf of Oman, which opens into the Arabian Sea. Iran covers 635,932 square miles (1,647,064 square kilometers), making it slightly larger than the state of Alaska.

A village sits nestled along the mountain slopes near Mount Damavand.

Mountainous Land

A large plateau sits in central Iran, but much of the rest of the country is mountainous. In fact, most Iranians live within view of a mountain range. Most people live in the foothills near the mountains because it rains more there, and water is precious in this arid country. These areas also have abundant small streams and lakes created by rain and melted mountain snow.

The Zagros Mountains form the main mountain chain in Iran. The ridges of the Zagros Range run northwest to southeast for about 930 miles (1,500 km). The highest point is Zard Kuh, which rises to 14,921 feet (4,548 meters). The peaks are lower farther south.

The Elburz Mountains cover most of northern Iran. This range includes Iran's highest mountain, the dormant volcano Mount Damavand, which rises to 18,934 feet (5,771 m) above

The Zagros Mountains dominate western Iran. Deep valleys and canyons cut through the mountains.

Iran's Geographic Features

Area: 635,932 square miles (1,647,064 sq km)

Highest Point: Mount Damavand, 18,934 feet high (5,771 m)

Lowest Point: Caspian Sea coast, 92 feet (28 m) below sea level

Average Temperatures:
Tehran: 35°F (2°C) in January; 85°F (29°C) in July
Khuzistan Plain: 54°F (12°C) in January; 97°F (36°C) in July

Longest River:
Karun, 528 miles (850 km)

Largest Lake: Urumia, the size varies, but is about 2,000 square miles (5,200 sq km)

Longest Mountain Range:
Zagros, 930 miles (1,500 km)

Largest Desert: Dasht-e Kavir, 30,000 square miles (77,600 sq km)

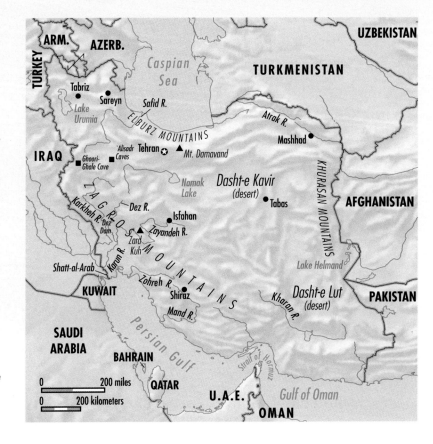

sea level. The towering peaks in the Elburz Mountains are popular with mountain climbers.

Eastern Iran is home to the Khurasan Mountains. The region around the mountains is also called Khurasan, which means "where the sun rises." The Sasanians, who ruled Iran more than 1,500 years ago, gave the region this name. Many valuable natural resources have been found in Khurasan, including turquoise, salt, iron, copper, lead, zinc, chromium, and coal.

Deserts

Most of the middle part of Iran consists of two vast deserts, the Dasht-e Kavir and the Dasht-e Lut. The Dasht-e Kavir, Iran's largest desert, lies in the north-central part of the country. It is covered with a crunchy crust of salt crystals. The salt layer forms when salty streams from the highlands run down and pool on dry desert land. The water quickly evaporates in the heat, leaving the salt behind. The Dasht-e Lut, on the other hand, is a sandy desert.

Few people live in the desolate Dasht-e Kavir.

On Shaky Ground

Earth's outer layer is divided up into several huge chunks called tectonic plates. Areas that lie on the boundaries between these plates are prone to earthquakes. Three tectonic plates meet in Iran, and tremors are common in the country. In the past hundred years, Iran has had twenty massive earthquakes. Here are the most recent major quakes:

1990: The worst earthquake on record hit Iran's Caspian region. Thirty-five thousand people died, and half a million were left homeless.

2003: The ancient city of Bam was nearly destroyed (left). Forty-three thousand people died, thirty thousand were injured, and more than seventy-five thousand lost their homes.

2005: An earthquake in central Iran shook more than forty villages, killing at least 612 people and injuring more than 1,400.

Almost no rain falls in Iran's deserts, and in the summer, temperatures sometimes top 120 degrees Fahrenheit (50 degrees Celsius). Few people live in the desert regions. Those who do settle around oases—places in the desert with underground springs. The springs allow people and plants to survive.

Thousands of years ago, desert people in the region built underground water systems called *qanats*. These underground canals tap into the natural water supply. They then take advantage of gravity to bring the water where it is needed. Modern water systems around the world are based on this ancient technology. Qanats are still used in Iran, Afghanistan, and throughout central Asia.

Frost carpets a sand dune in the Dasht e-Kavir. In the winter, nighttime temperatures often drop below freezing.

Oasis Life

Tabas is a group of small villages in an oasis between the Dasht-e Kavir and the Dasht-e Lut. Lush trees, public gardens, and cool pools make this historic region a real treat in the middle of the desert. About thirty thousand people live in Tabas. Many tourists visit Tabas to enjoy the greenery and explore the ruins of an ancient fortress.

The Lowlands

A narrow stretch of lowland lies along the southern coast of the Caspian Sea. It is one of Iran's most fertile regions. The Khuzistan Plain, to the north of the Persian Gulf, is both important agriculturally and rich in oil.

The Caspian Sea borders northern Iran. Its water is salty, but not as salty as ocean water.

The Bridge of Thirty-Three Arches spans the Zayandeh River in Isfahan. It was built in 1602.

Precious Water

Iran has three major rivers, the Karun, the Zayandeh, and the Safid. The Karun is the only river in Iran large enough to carry boats. It is the nation's longest river, flowing more than 500 miles (800 km) from the Zagros Mountains to the Iraqi border, where it joins the Shatt-al-Arab and empties into the Persian Gulf. Shipping is important on the lower part of the river because it flows through a major oil region. A dam constructed in 1971 diverts water from the Karun through a long tunnel into the Zayandeh River. This river supplies water to the ancient city of Isfahan. The Safid River begins in the Elburz Mountains in the north and flows into the Caspian Sea.

Other rivers in Iran come and go with the seasons. In the summer, most of them dry up completely. After spring rains, these rivers sometimes flood, producing extensive damage. Iran also has seasonal lakes, many of which are salty.

Lake Urumia, in northwestern Iran, is the country's largest lake. It covers about 2,000 square miles (5,200 sq km). Like many lakes in Iran, it has mineral-rich waters. Some people believe that bathing in Urumia's waters can cure disease and soothe the soul. Iran also has both hot and cold mineral springs, where water bubbles up from underground. The town of Sareyn has developed a spa resort around the area's hot springs.

Looking at Iran's Cities

The largest city in Iran by far is the capital, Tehran, with about 14 million people. Iran's next-largest city is Mashhad, with about 2 million people. Mashhad, a center of industry and trade, lies in northeastern Iran. It is sometimes called Iran's holiest city because it is the site of the Imam Reza Shrine (below). Imam Reza, a leader of Shi'i Islam in the ninth century, was killed in Mashhad. Every year, millions of people visit his tomb.

Tabriz, the largest city in northwestern Iran, has about 1.7 million people. Tabriz has a rich history. It served as the capital several times between 1250 and 1550 and was also an artistic center. Its major sites include the Ark, a huge fortress built in the 1300s. Tabriz's Blue Mosque is famous for its tile work. Much of the mosque was destroyed in an earthquake in 1778, but it has been reconstructed.

About 1 million people live in Isfahan (above), which sits in the foothills of the Zagros Mountains. Isfahan is a center of industry, and carpets, steel, and handicrafts are produced there. Isfahan is renowned for its broad streets, lush gardens, and splendid palaces and mosques. Naqsh-i Jahan Square, at the center of Isfahan, is one of the world's largest squares. It is lined with historic buildings, including the Ali Qapu Palace and the Shah Mosque.

Sea or Lake?

Iran shares the Caspian Sea with Russia, Turkmenistan, Azerbaijan, and Kazakhstan. These countries formed the Caspian Cooperation Organization in order to better share and preserve the Caspian's resources. One question they have debated is whether to continue to call the Caspian a sea or to reclassify it as a lake. The difference has important political and economic consequences. According to international law, the resources of a lake must be shared equally with all bordering countries. If the Caspian is a sea, each country gets a particular slice of territory. Classification as a sea is a huge advantage for some countries because oil has been found under their slices of the Caspian. Azerbaijan and Kazakhstan have more than 80 percent of the expected

Caspian oil reserves. Iran has very little oil in this region but does hold vast oil reserves elsewhere.

Iran's northern border touches the Caspian Sea. Stretching across 143,550 square miles (371,795 sq km), this salty body of water is the world's largest inland sea.

Hot and Cold

The climate varies significantly in different parts of Iran. The north and the west experience four distinct seasons. In the south and the east, spring and fall are short, and there are long, hot summers and mild winters.

Ski resorts in the Elburz Mountains near Tehran provide people with an escape from crowded city life. Those who dislike the cold head south for the winter, to the islands and warm breezes along the Persian Gulf.

Most of Iran is generally dry. The main exception is the Caspian coast, where it rains throughout the year. Precipitation (rain and snow) varies widely across the country, ranging from less than 2 inches (5 centimeters) a year in the southeast to about 80 inches (200 cm) in the Caspian region. The fertile valleys between mountain ridges often get 40 inches (100 cm) of rain per year. This makes them desirable places to live.

Warm, damp winds typically blow in from the Persian Gulf all year. In the winter, cold winds also blow down from the north. Come summer, winds whip through Iran with speeds of up to 70 miles (115 km) per hour. These winds can turn sand into a deadly weapon. But industrious desert-dwelling Iranians capture the wind in giant wind towers called *badgirs*, which funnel the cool air into buildings.

Clouds gather over the Caspian Sea. The Caspian region is the wettest part of Iran.

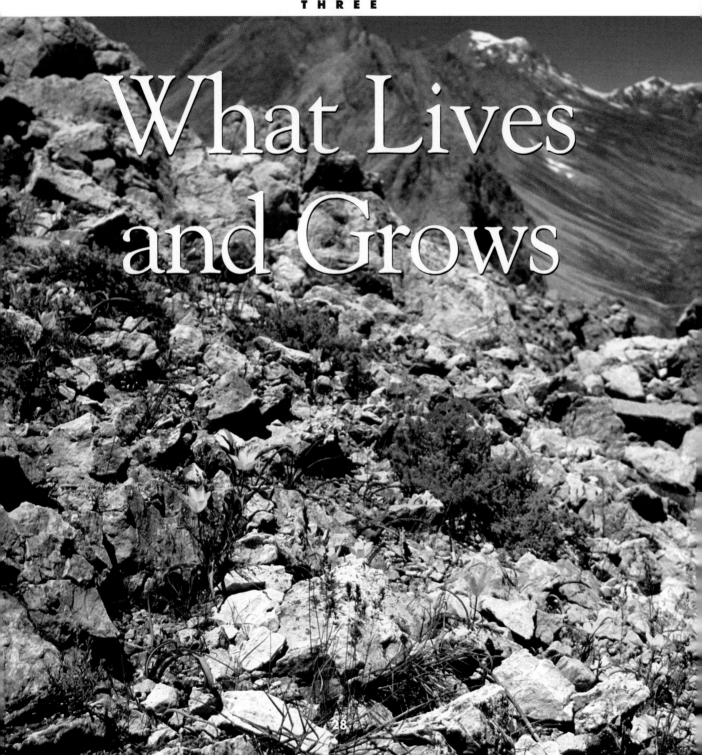

What Lives and Grows

About 10 percent of Iran is forested. Most of the forests are in the north, near the Caspian Sea. At one time, much more of the country was forested. But many trees have been cut, and pollution has taken a toll. These changes rob plants and animals of their natural habitats. Many species are endangered, and some have gone extinct entirely.

Fortunately, Iran has some national parks where endangered species, if carefully protected, can thrive again. But environmental laws need to be better enforced to ensure that the animals survive.

Iran is home to a wide variety of animals, including frogs. Here, a marsh frog swims with its vocal sacs inflated.

Opposite: Wild tulips dot the rugged mountain slopes near Tehran.

Mouflon, a type of wild sheep, live in Iran's arid mountains.

Wildlife

Iran's oldest national park is in Golestan, in the north of the country. This mountainous region provides a variety of habitats for animals such as leopards, gazelles, wild sheep, ibex, and wild boars.

Iran is home to the last of the endangered Asiatic cheetahs. Experts believe there are only fifty to one hundred of these animals left in the wild. They live in the desert and dry shrub lands. They share the area with wild sheep, wild goats, sand foxes, striped hyenas, wolves, and hares. Iran is working to save the Asiatic cheetah from extinction. The nation has set aside 14,750 square miles (38,200 sq km) specifically for the Asiatic cheetah.

More common animals in Iran include deer and squirrels. Nearly a hundred species of lizards live in Iran. In 2000, scientists discovered a new species, the blue-tailed lizard,

Africa in Iran

Kavir National Park covers a rugged part of northern Iran that has few plants but some thorny trees. This park is sometimes called Little Africa because it supports the kind of animals that people expect to see in Africa. These include Iranian species, such as the rare Asiatic cheetah and the Persian panther, as well as gazelles and hyenas.

which they believe lives only in Iran. The blue-tailed lizard was found near the city of Yassuj. In the Lar Valley of the Elburz Mountains, researchers have also found Latifi vipers, venomous snakes found only in that valley. Identifying spe-

Iran is home to many kinds of lizards, including skinks.

cies like these is an important step toward protecting the variety of life on earth.

Iran has more than 390 species of butterflies. Many of them live in the Zagros and the Elburz mountains. Butterflies don't live long. Some live only a week, while others survive a few months. The biggest threat to Iranian butterflies is overgrazing by cattle, which destroys the pastures where butterflies live.

About five hundred different bird species have been seen in Iran. Some live there year-round. Others just pass through in the course of their seasonal migrations. Migratory waterbirds include the pink great flamingo, which is frequently seen around Lake Urumia, in northwestern Iran. Brine shrimp and small crabs are among the few living things in this salty lake, and brine shrimp are a favorite food of the flamingos.

More than a hundred small, rocky islands pepper Lake Urumia. These islands are home to a variety of birds, including

Lake Urumia in northwestern Iran is an important breeding ground for great flamingos. The lake is home to an estimated twenty-five thousand breeding pairs of flamingos.

pelicans, storks, ibises, and sheldrakes. Many of the same birds stop at the coastal wetlands along the Caspian Sea.

The golden eagle is sometimes seen near the Caspian. This magnificent bird of prey has a wingspan of 6 to 7 feet (1.8 to 2.1 m) and weighs 8 to 12 pounds (3.6 to 5.4 kilograms). Birds seen in the mountains of Iran include the kingfisher, the imperial eagle, the black vulture, and the Siberian crane.

Golden eagles prey on hares, mice, and other small animals. They use their powerful talons to kill and carry their prey.

Hawksbill turtles nest on islands along Iran's coast. The turtle gets its name from its curved, pointed head that looks like a bird's beak.

Sea Life

The waters around Iran support trout, herring, mullet, salmon, and tuna. Coral reefs sit in the warm, shallow waters off Iran's southern coast. These formations are made from the skeletons of countless tiny creatures called coral polyps. Living corals are colorful and often have soft, flexible shapes.

Lobsters, shrimps, sea urchins, and many types of bright tropical fish live in the warm waters near the reefs. Unfortunately,

Tulips for Honor

The tulip holds a special place in Iranian culture. Tulips are popular in Iranian gardens, and they are often mentioned in poems and stories. In Iran, the tulip is a symbol of martyrdom, or dying for a cause. According to Iranian myth, if a young soldier dies fighting for Iran, a red tulip will grow on his grave.

pollution, much of it caused by the oil industry, is a constant threat to Iran's marine life.

Trees, Shrubs, and Flowers

Most of Iran is dry, so plants that live there are well adapted to life with little moisture. Prickly shrubs and short grasses survive in the deserts. Desert oases, which have more water, support many trees, including date palm, myrtle, oleander, acacia, willow, elm, plum, and mulberry.

A hardy willow tree grows in central Iran. Most Iranian willows grow in oases, ravines, or along the damp Caspian coast.

Most of the nation's forests are on the shores of the Caspian Sea. Trees such as oak, beech, linden, elm, walnut, and ash grow in these forests, as do thorny shrubs and ferns.

Elm, maple, walnut, pear, and pistachio trees grow in the Zagros Mountains. Willow and poplar trees take root in ravines. Some varieties of juniper and wild fruit trees grow on the dry plateaus. Wildflowers create carpets of color in the mountains, especially in spring and early summer. These flowers include buttercups, geraniums, irises, orchids, and wild roses.

Through the Ages

THE FIRST KNOWN CIVILIZATION IN WHAT IS NOW IRAN was that of the Elamites, who settled around the northern Persian Gulf in about 3000 B.C. The Elamites had a strong system of government, a military, and organized systems of trade. Some Elamites could read and write. They used the cuneiform writing system, which they adopted from people who lived in a region known as Mesopotamia, in what is now Iraq. Today, the remains of an Elamite temple, Chogha Zanbil, are still visible in Susa, in southwestern Iran.

Opposite: **Susa was the capital of the ancient Elamite civilization. Parts of ancient Susa have been excavated.**

Chogha Zanbil is a religious site in western Iran. It was built in about 1250 B.C.

What's in a Name?

The name *Iran* comes from the term *Aryan* (AIR-ee-an), which means "the Noble." In 1500 B.C., the Aryans settled in the area known today as Iran. Their descendants were the Medes and the Persians. The Medes lived to the north, while the Persians settled farther south. Eventually, the Persians conquered the Medes and the whole territory became known as the Persian Empire. The country was called Persia until 1935, when Reza Shah Pahlavi officially changed its name to Iran.

The Aryans made their way into the region around 1500 B.C. They are thought to have migrated from central Asia. They settled in lands called Pars or Parsa, and they became known as Persians. As was common at this time, political power was passed down from generation to generation within families. These families are called dynasties. Family members often fought among themselves to control the territory.

The Achaemenid Dynasty

A Persian king named Achaemenes established the Achaemenid dynasty in what is now southern Iran. The dynasty reached its greatest glory under the rule of Cyrus the Great. Cyrus became king in 580 B.C., at age twenty-one, and ruled until 529 B.C. Cyrus waged war against the Medes, who

The Cyrus Cylinder

Cyrus the Great had his ethical code written down for all to see. It is written in cuneiform on a clay cylinder that is known as the Cyrus Cylinder. It includes the statement, "I forbid slavery, and my governors and subordinates are obliged to prohibit exchanging men and women as slaves within their own ruling domains. Such a tradition should be exterminated the world over."

Some people call the Cyrus Cylinder the first charter of human rights. It is now on display at the British Museum in London, England.

lived to the north. He united the Medes and the Persians to create the first Persian Empire.

Among Cyrus's greatest achievements was the capture of Babylon, a powerful city in Mesopotamia, in 539 B.C. Jewish people had been enslaved in Babylon. Cyrus thought slavery was immoral, so after conquering Babylon, he gave the Jewish people the freedom to return to their homes.

Darius I, another great ruler, took control in 521 B.C. During his reign, the Persian Empire expanded farther than ever before or since. At the time, it was the world's largest empire. It stretched east into India and central Asia; north to the Caucasus; and as far west as the Nile River in Egypt.

Darius built magnificent palaces and highways to connect different parts of the empire. Messengers would ride from station to station along these highways carrying important orders from the king, in what could be called one of the world's first postal systems. The Greek historian Herodotus later wrote about the Persian postal process, "Neither snow nor rain nor heat nor darkness of night prevents them from accomplishing the task proposed to them with the very utmost speed." Today, a version of this quote is an unofficial motto of the U.S. Postal Service.

Darius I began many building projects, most famously the palace complex of Persepolis. This sculpture of Darius appears on a wall at Persepolis.

Darius conquered parts of India and tried to make his way into mainland Greece. But he met his match in Greece in 490 B.C. at the Battle of Marathon, where he was forced to retreat.

The Remains of an Empire

In 518 B.C., Darius began to build Persepolis, one of the most magnificent sites in the ancient world. The vast palace complex included temples, government buildings, and a place for special ceremonies. This fabulous monument took more than two hundred years to complete. Its many carvings were once covered in gold, bronze, and lapis lazuli. Today, nothing is left but the stone underneath, but it is still remarkable. The ruins of Persepolis are among the most visited historical sites in Iran.

The Empire Declines

After Darius died in 486 B.C., his son Xerxes ruled Persia. Xerxes was angry about the defeat at Marathon, so he invaded Greece with an army of more than two hundred thousand. His forces launched their attack at the Hellespont, a narrow stretch of sea that separates Asia from Europe. To cross the Hellespont, Xerxes put boats side by side to form a bridge. Before the battle, he poured wine into the water in hopes of gaining strength from the gods. Maybe it helped, for Xerxes did succeed in taking some Greek land. He was defeated at sea, however. The Greek ships were sturdier, and they destroyed the Persian fleet. This defeat marked the beginning of the slow decline of the first Persian Empire.

Xerxes' troops invaded Greece by building a bridge of boats across the Hellespont.

Alexander the Great, who came from the northern Greek kingdom of Macedonia, invaded Persia in 330 B.C. He destroyed much of the famed palace complex at Persepolis, although it was not his intention to destroy all things Persian. In fact, he fell in love with a Persian princess named Roxana, whom he married. He wanted to unite Persians and Greeks, so he convinced thousands of his soldiers to marry Persian women.

Seleucids and Parthians

Alexander died in 323 B.C., at the age of thirty-three. Because he had not appointed anyone to take over after his death, three of his generals split his empire among themselves. One of them,

Alexander the Great is considered one of the greatest military commanders of all time. In just thirteen years, he conquered territory from Greece to India and south into Egypt.

The Silk Road

From about the second century B.C., the main trade route across Asia was the Silk Road. It stretched 5,000 miles (8,000 km), from India and China to the Mediterranean Sea. The Silk Road was not really one road but, rather, a web of many roads. People transported silk, jewelry, spices, pottery, perfumes, and more along the route.

Ideas and knowledge about different cultures were also exchanged along the way. For example, as traders traveled back and forth along the Silk Road, they learned about such diverse religions and philosophies as Zoroastrianism, Buddhism, Christianity, Judaism, and Confucianism.

Seleucus, took over Iran. In time, the Seleucids would control territory from what is now Turkey all the way to India. The Seleucid Empire lasted until 250 B.C. While the Seleucids were in power, Greek and Persian culture mingled.

Civil wars eventually weakened the Seleucid Empire. The Parthians, who lived in the north along the Caspian Sea, wrested control from the Selucids. They were related to both Persians and Greeks. The Parthians ruled from 250 B.C. until A.D. 224. They did little to expand the territory of the empire, but they did a lot in the name of art and culture.

The Parthians developed styles of art and architecture that borrowed ideas from the Greeks. The distinctive Parthian architectural style includes the *iwan*, a hall that has walls on three sides and an open archway at one end. The iwan has

A magnificent palace was built at Ctesiphon for Khosrau I. All that remains of it today are one wall and a grand archway.

become a trademark of Islamic architecture and is now seen all over the Middle East.

The Sasanians

The Parthians were overthrown by the Sasanians, who established the second Persian Empire. The Sasanians ruled most of what is now Iran from 224 to 642. Their capital was at Ctesiphon, in an area that is now part of Iraq. The most famous Sasanian king was Khosrau I, who was also called Anushirvan the Just. He was considered just because he reformed the tax system, making it fairer to poor farmers. He also built new towns and helped restart farms that had been ruined by war. The official religion of the Sasanian Empire was Zoroastrianism, but Khosrau tolerated other religions. In fact, his own son became a Christian.

Khosrau died in 579, and the rulers who followed him didn't continue his policies. Instead, they increased taxes on the poor. As a result, peasant farmers rose up in revolt. There was chaos in the countryside. The economy declined, and the empire became vulnerable. New invaders would soon take advantage of this weakness. It was perfect timing for the Arabs, whose army was steadily making its way toward Iran.

The Arabs and Islam

An Arab army entered Iran from the southwest in the 630s. The Arabs are especially significant in the region's history because they brought with them the religion of Islam. At the time of the Arab invasion, many of the region's Zoroastrian religious leaders were corrupt. The Iranians were ready for some-

During the Seljuk period, many tomb towers were built in Iran. The body lay in a coffin on the first floor, while the upper floor served as a chapel.

thing new. Islam stressed equality and justice. It gave people hope that their lives would improve. By about A.D. 1000, most Iranians had converted to Islam.

The Arabs ruled Iran until they were conquered by the Seljuks in the middle of the eleventh century. The Seljuks were a Turkish people originally from central Asia. In time, they would be ousted by the Mongols, invaders from farther east.

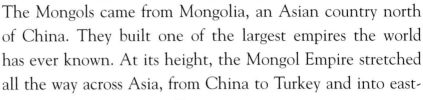

Mongol Invasions

The Mongols came from Mongolia, an Asian country north of China. They built one of the largest empires the world has ever known. At its height, the Mongol Empire stretched all the way across Asia, from China to Turkey and into eastern Europe.

The Mongols first stormed across Iran in 1220. They were brutal invaders, sometimes destroying entire cities. They also damaged crops and ruined the underground water systems called qanats.

The Mongols gradually fell under the influence of the peoples whom they conquered. In 1295, Ghazan Khan, the ruler of the western part of the Mongol lands, converted to Islam to gain more support from the local people. Ghazan Khan also improved the Iranian economy, rebuilt the qanats, and fostered trade. Mongol domination faded by 1501. The time was ripe for the next great Persian empire to rise.

Genghis Khan built a vast empire. When he died in 1227, his empire spread across Asia from the Pacific Ocean to what is now eastern Iran.

The Safavids

The third Persian Empire was founded by a young man named Ismail Safavi. His army became the strongest in Iran.

By 1502, at the age of fifteen, he had unified Iran and become shah, the ruler of the region. After centuries of outside rule, power was back in Persian hands. Ismail also made Shi'i Islam the state religion of Persia.

The greatest Safavid shah was Abbas the Great, who ruled from 1587 to 1629. He helped restore the Persian Empire to its former glory. Shah Abbas had religious schools and palaces built. He also improved the economy through trade with the British and the Dutch. He hired skilled craftspeople to design carpets, and Persian carpets were soon among the luxuries Europeans most desired. But his crowning achievement was the completion of Isfahan, the Safavids' new capital. Isfahan was filled with wide avenues and lush gardens. Today, this jewel of a city is home to nearly two million people, and it is a top tourist destination. Isfahan is a rare world treasure.

Ismail Safavi united Iran under the Safavid dynasty when he was still a teenager.

The original Peacock Throne was destroyed in the 1740s. Later Iranian thrones, such as the Naderi Throne shown here, are also sometimes called the Peacock Throne.

Nadir Shah

After Abbas the Great's death, the Safavids faded. In 1722, the Afghans invaded Iran, but their rule did not last long. Soon, a military genius named Nadir Shah drove them out. He became shah in 1736.

Nadir Shah soon began expanding Persia's borders once again. He won battles against the Russians and the Turks. He also marched south into India, where he stole many valuable treasures, including the Koh-i Noor diamond and the Peacock Throne. The Peacock Throne was encrusted with more than twenty thousand diamonds, rubies, emeralds, and other jewels.

Nadir Shah is remembered as both a great military leader and a cruel and oppressive ruler. He was far more interested in expanding his lands than in improving the welfare of his people. In 1747, he was killed by one of his own commanders.

The Qajar Dynasty

The next notable dynasty, the Qajar dynasty, lasted from 1794 to 1925. The Qajars moved the capital to Tehran, where it has remained.

In the early 1800s, the Qajars found themselves in the middle of a political rivalry. The Russians wanted access to the Persian Gulf because their own northern ports were frozen over during the winter. At the time, Great Britain controlled most of India. The British were afraid that the Russians might interfere with their trade route through the Persian Gulf. The British wanted Iran to act as a friendly buffer state between them and the Russians.

Iran stood between two powerful forces. Because the Qajars needed money, they made deals with both countries. Both the British and the Russians established banks in Iran. They both started mining in Iran, and they both tried to gain control of Iranian industries. The Qajar shahs grew wealthy from their deals with the foreigners, while the Iranian economy declined. The Iranian people grew angry at this state of affairs.

Ahmad Shah was the last leader of the Qajar dynasty. He came to power when he was just eleven years old.

Unrest increased, and in 1906, the Iranian people forced the shah to draw up a constitution. For the first time, Iran would have an elected legislature, the Majlis.

Then, in 1908, oil was discovered in Iran. The Anglo-Persian Oil Company began building refineries along the Persian Gulf. In 1914, the British government took over the company. Oil would soon become Iran's main source of income. But most of the profits went to the British.

Oil production began in Iran in 1913. The country sits on top of about 9 percent of the world's oil reserves.

Reza Shah Pahlavi began his career as an army officer. During his years as Iran's ruler, he introduced many reforms.

The Pahlavi Dynasty

World War I created new problems. Though Iran wasn't directly involved in the war, Russians fought Turks in the northeastern part of the country. British troops, meanwhile, were sent to protect the oil fields in the south. In 1923, a general named Reza Khan overthrew the last Qajar ruler. Reza Khan's family name was Pahlavi. In 1925, he took the title of shah, becoming Reza Shah Pahlavi.

Reza Shah tried to modernize Iran. He reduced the power of the clergy. He demanded that Iranians wear western clothes. Women could no longer wear a veil or a long black robe called a *chador*. Men wore suits instead of traditional Iranian clothes.

Reza Shah created a national education system and opened the University of Tehran, where scholars from Europe came to teach. He also hired technical experts from Europe to help build the Trans-Iranian Railway, a railroad that crosses the country. Iran was well on its way to becoming a modern state.

In 1941, Reza Shah Pahlavi was forced out of power. His twenty-one year old son, Mohammad Reza (center), replaced him as shah.

World War II broke out in 1939, and once again Iran was in a difficult position. Three of the main countries involved in the war—Britain, the Soviet Union (a large country made up of Russia and other nearby states), and Germany—were all important to Iran. But Britain and the Soviet Union were fighting Germany. Reza Shah had some sympathy for Germany, Iran's main trading partner. In 1941, the Soviets and the British forced him to give up the throne in favor of his son Mohammad Reza.

Early on, Mohammad Reza was heavily influenced by the British, who were still in control of the Anglo-Iranian Oil Company, as it was now known. Most of the money produced by Iran's oil industry continued to go to the British. In 1951, Iranian politician Muhammad Musaddiq spoke out against the oil industry agreements. He believed that Iranians deserved a larger share of the profits. Many people agreed, and the Iranian government nationalized the oil industry.

This, of course, did not please the British. In 1953, they began a boycott of Iranian oil. The nation's oil production also dropped, and many people lost their jobs. Supporters of Musaddiq, who was by then prime minister, fought supporters of Mohammad Reza Shah. Eventually, the shah fled the country.

The British, however, had convinced the United States to help them remove Musaddiq from office. He was forced out, and Mohammad Reza Shah returned. The oil industry was denationalized, although the British no longer controlled it all. About 40 percent of the Iranian oil industry was now in the hands of the United States.

Like his father, the shah wanted to modernize the country. He built schools, hospitals, and roads. But as time went on, he also grew more and more dictatorial. Some clerics (religious leaders) saw his changes as a threat to Islam. Other Iranians believed the shah was corrupt. They wanted genuine and democratic reform. The shah outlawed all political parties but his own. Those who spoke out against him were imprisoned. Some were killed. Meanwhile, agricultural production fell, and prices soared. Opposition to the shah's rule grew. Huge protests against the shah became common.

Ayatollah Ruhollah Khomeini began publicly denouncing the shah's policies as early as 1963. He became the leader of those opposing the shah.

A Muslim leader named Ayatollah Ruhollah Khomeini was one of the shah's most vocal opponents. He condemned the shah for being corrupt and in the pocket of the United States. Many Iranians rallied to the ayatollah's message.

The Islamic Revolution

Facing massive discontent, the shah fled Iran on January 16, 1979. This event is now celebrated as a national holiday. Within weeks, Ayatollah Khomeini took control of the country.

Khomeini declared that Iran was an Islamic republic. He advocated the idea that the clergy must rule. This was Khomeini's own innovation rather than part of traditional Islam.

Mohammad Reza Shah (right) left Iran in 1979. He died the following year.

Khomeini ruled with an iron fist. Many people who had worked with the shah were put to death. Women were forced to cover their hair and wear chadors. The University of Tehran was closed for two years. Newspapers were shut down, and history books rewritten. Girls and boys could no longer attend class together. Women could not be seen in public with men unless they were family members.

In October 1979, President Jimmy Carter allowed Mohammad Reza Shah to enter the United States to be treated for cancer. This infuriated Iranians. Soon, Iranian students stormed the U.S. embassy in Tehran and took more than fifty people hostage. They demanded that the shah be sent back to Iran to stand trial, but the United States refused. The hostages were held for more than a year.

Then, in the summer of 1980, Iraq invaded Iran. The reason was supposedly a border dispute. But in fact, Saddam Hussein, the ruler of Iraq, thought he would easily be able to bring down the new Iranian regime because of the chaos in the country. The war lasted eight long years. Cities were damaged. Oil facilities were destroyed. More than a million people were killed in the two countries. Finally, a cease-fire was declared in 1988.

An Iraqi soldier on the front-lines during the Iran-Iraq War. Early in the war, Iraq captured the Iranian port city of Khorramshahr, but soon the war settled into a long stalemate.

Muhammad Khatami won nearly 70 percent of the vote in the presidential election of 1997.

When Ayatollah Khomeini died in 1989, millions of people mourned in the streets. For many Iranians who do not want to see Iran dominated by the West, he remains a hero. Many thousands of people visit his shrine every year.

Following Khomeini's death, Sayyid Ali Khamenei took over as Iran's spiritual and political leader. In the years since, Iran has moved in a more moderate direction. Enforcement of some of the strict laws enacted during Khomeini's time has relaxed.

A moderate cleric by the name of Ayatollah Muhammad Khatami won the presidential election in 1997. He was reelected in 2001 by a wide margin. President Khatami hoped to improve the status of women and give more people a voice in how Iran is governed. He was also friendlier to the West than prior presidents had been. But Khatami was unable to accomplish much. Throughout his time in office, he repeatedly ran up against other more conservative and powerful government leaders who did not share his goals.

In 2005, Mahmoud Ahmadinejad, the former mayor of Tehran, won the presidency. He turned Iran in a more conservative direction.

Iran continues to have strained relations with the West, especially the United States. Iran's nuclear program has particularly raised concerns. Iran's need for electricity is soaring. Iranian officials say they are simply trying to develop nuclear energy, but many people believe they are actually trying to make nuclear weapons. Who is being truthful? The question remains unanswered.

President Mahmoud Ahmadinejad has made many confrontational statements. In 2005, he said that the Jewish state of Israel should be destroyed.

FIVE

The Islamic Republic

58

Women in Iran are required to cover their hair. Some cover their entire body.

I N 1979, IRAN BECAME THE WORLD'S FIRST ISLAMIC REPUBLIC. The government is run according to the Iranian leaders' interpretations of Shi'i Islam.

All citizens, whether Muslim or not (only about 1 percent of the population is non-Muslim), are required by law to follow Islamic rules. Thus, alcohol is forbidden. Women must wear head scarves and cannot serve in the judiciary. Yet according to the Iranian government's interpretation of Shi'i Islam, women can vote and hold public office. In fact, women's votes were vital in electing the moderate cleric Muhammad Khatami president in 1997 and 2001.

Opposite: **Iranian women were granted the right to vote in 1963.**

Iran's supreme leader, Ayatollah Sayyid Ali Khamenei, is considered a conservative. He was an important figure in the Islamic Revolution.

NATIONAL GOVERNMENT OF IRAN

Executive Branch

SUPREME LEADER

COUNCIL OF GUARDIANS

PRESIDENT

Legislative Branch

MAJLIS

Judicial Branch

SUPREME COURT

LOWER COURTS

REVOLUTIONARY COURTS

Government Structure

Iran adopted a new constitution in 1979, in the aftermath of the Islamic Revolution. The constitution set up a complicated government structure including both elected and appointed officials. The government is divided into three branches: executive, legislative, and judicial.

Ultimate power lies in the hands of the supreme leader. The supreme leader must be a well-educated Islamic scholar. He is appointed for life by the Assembly of Experts, a group of eighty-six clerics whose members are elected to eight-year terms.

Although the supreme leader does not run the day-to-day affairs of the country, he sets the tone for everything. The supreme leader has the power to reject anything the president or legislature proposes. He appoints military officers, clerical members of the Council of Guardians, members of the judiciary, and the head of Iran's radio and television networks. The supreme leader is the commander in chief of the military, the only person who can declare war or peace. After the death of Ayatollah Ruhollah Khomeini in 1989, Sayyid Ali Khamenei became the supreme leader of Iran.

The National Anthem

After Ayatollah Khomeini died in 1989, Iran held a competition to write a new national anthem. The anthem, written by Hassan Riahi, was adopted in 1990.

Upwards on the horizon rises the Eastern Sun,
The sight of the true Religion.
Bahman—the brilliance of our Faith.
Your message, O Imam, of independence and freedom
is imprinted on our souls.
O Martyrs! The time of your cries of pain rings in our ears.
Enduring, continuing, eternal,
The Islamic Republic of Iran.

Most important political leaders in Iran are clerics.

The president, who is the head of state, must be an Iranian-born Shi'i Muslim. He is elected by popular vote to a four-year term and can serve two terms in a row. (Anyone age eighteen or older can vote.) The president's duties include appointing cabinet members, carrying out foreign policy, and maintaining the country's economic health.

The supreme leader has much more power than the president, making the democratic process questionable. For example, Muhammad Khatami was elected president in 1997 with 78 percent of the vote. Khatami tried to reform and modernize the country, and most Iranians wanted such changes. But the country's conservative forces were able to block many of his efforts because they were backed by the supreme leader. In 2005, Khatami lost reelection to the conservative Mahmoud Ahmadinejad.

Mahmoud Ahmadinejad

President Mahmoud Ahmadinejad was born in a village southeast of Tehran in 1956. He studied civil engineering in college and received a doctorate in engineering in 1987.

During the Iran-Iraq War, Ahmadinejad served with the Islamic Revolutionary Guard Corps. Later, he became involved in politics. He served as governor of West Azerbaijan Province and was an adviser to the Ministry of Culture and Higher Education in 1993. From 2003 to 2005, he served as mayor of Tehran. During his time as mayor, he reversed many moderate and reformist policies put into place by previous mayors.

Ahmadinejad was elected president in 2005. Deeply conservative, he has vowed to return Iran to more traditional Islamic ways.

The legislature, or Majlis, has 290 members who are elected to four-year terms. They write and enact laws, ratify treaties, and approve the budget. They can also impeach (remove) the president. The Majlis is overseen by the twelve-member Council of Guardians. The council reviews all laws proposed by the Majlis to make sure they comply with Islamic principles. If the council deems a law unacceptable, it can either reject it entirely or send it back to the Majlis for revision. The Council of Guardians also has the power to reject any candidate running for political office, including the presidency.

Five seats in the Iranian legislature are reserved for religious minorities.

اظهارات تحت فشار روحی ی اعتبار است.

دفاع علنی میخواهد

م علنی ناروا ا

دادگاه سیاسی پشت درهای بسته

بازجویی پنهانی سلول پنهانی

Families of people arrested for calling for more openness and tolerance in Iranian society demonstrate outside Tehran's revolutionary court. They hold signs protesting the revolutionary court's secret trials.

Courts and the Law

Iran's judiciary includes a supreme court and a series of lower courts that deal with criminal and civil disputes. The supreme leader basically controls the courts. He appoints the head of the judiciary, and that person appoints the head of the Supreme Court. Iran also has revolutionary courts, which handle cases that are seen as particularly offensive to Islamic law. These include drug smuggling and acts that threaten national security. Decisions made in revolutionary courts cannot be appealed to the Supreme Court.

The revolution of 1979 brought back some violent historical punishments. For example, someone caught stealing may have a hand cut off, people who drink alcohol may be flogged (severely whipped), and a person accused of adultery may be stoned to death. In practice, apart from flogging, such sentences have rarely been carried out.

Local Government

Iran is divided into thirty provinces, which are further divided into counties, districts, and townships. A governor, who is appointed by the national government, leads each province. Each province also has a council, whose members are elected by the people in the province.

A meeting of the Assembly of Experts. The Assembly of Experts has the power to both elect and dismiss the supreme leader.

The National Flag

Iran's flag was adopted in 1980 following the Islamic Revolution. The flag has three horizontal bands of green, white, and red. In the middle is the national emblem, a stylized version of the word *Allah* ("God" in Arabic). *Allahu akbar* ("God is great") appears in white Arabic script eleven times along the bottom edge of the green band and eleven times along the top edge of the red band. This symbolizes that the revolution happened on the twenty-second day of the eleventh month in the Iranian calendar.

Military Might

All Iranian men are required to serve eighteen months in the military. Most serve in the nation's large army. Others serve in the navy, the air force, or the Islamic Revolutionary Guard Corps.

Iranian soldiers march in a ceremony in Tehran in 2006. Iran has more than half a million active members of the armed forces.

Young members of the Revolutionary Guard stand at attention. The Revolutionary Guard has its own ground forces, air force, navy, special forces, and militia.

The Revolutionary Guard was created by Ayatollah Khomeini to uphold the principles of the revolution. Its members are generally quite religious. In the early days of the revolution, the Revolutionary Guard acted as a vigilante police force who ensured that Iranians were obeying the new laws. They beat or arrested people for such crimes as drinking alcohol and dancing. The Revolutionary Guard has also been involved in conflicts in other countries. It has supported Shi'i movements in Palestine, Lebanon, and, Iraq.

Iran manufactures some of its own weapons but also buys many from China, North Korea, and Russia. Iran cannot buy weapons from the United States because the United States banned all weapons sales to Iran after American employees of the U.S. embassy were taken hostage in 1979. The ban is still in place.

Tehran: Did You Know This?

Tehran is the capital of Iran and the country's industrial, technological, and educational center. The beautiful Elburz Mountains form the backdrop to this modern city. Iranians love the city's many gardens, especially those with fountains or running water. There are also parks for relaxation and play.

Tehran is a bustling city. Dense traffic sends billows of smog into the already polluted air. High-rise buildings line the skyline, and air conditioners hang in windows. The city is filled with advertisements, some on large video screens, which promote products such as computers, fast food, and soft drinks.

Movie theaters, museums, Internet cafés, markets, teahouses, and restaurants provide plenty for visitors and Iranians to see and do. One of Tehran's highlights is the Carpet Museum, which has an impressive collection of Persian carpets. The Golestan ("Rose Garden") Palace (above), where leaders of the Qajar dynasty lived, is a cool, quiet getaway from the noise of the city. The National Jewels Museum displays a 182-carat pink diamond called the Sea of Light and the Naderi Throne, which is covered with 26,733 gems.

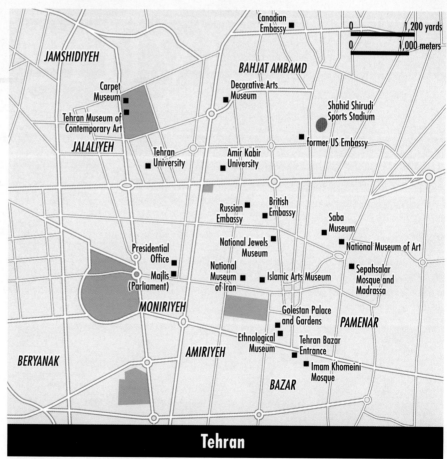

Canadian Embassy

0   1,200 yards
0   1,000 meters

JAMSHIDIYEH

BAHJAT AMBAMD

Carpet Museum

Decorative Arts Museum

Shahid Shirudi Sports Stadium

Tehran Museum of Contemporary Art

JALALIYEH

former US Embassy

Tehran University

Amir Kabir University

Russian Embassy

British Embassy

Saba Museum

National Museum of Art

Presidential Office

National Jewels Museum

Majlis (Parliament)

National Museum of Iran

Islamic Arts Museum

Sepahsalar Mosque and Madrassa

MONIRIYEH

Golestan Palace and Gardens

PAMENAR

BERYANAK

AMIRIYEH

Ethnological Museum

Tehran Bazar Entrance

Imam Khomeini Mosque

BAZAR

Tehran

Making a Living

THE AVERAGE IRANIAN EARNS THE EQUIVALENT OF ABOUT US$8,700 per year. Gas, electricity, housing, and other items are far cheaper in Iran than in the United States, however, so that amount of money buys more.

Many Iranians work six days a week. They take off only Friday, the day of rest in the Muslim tradition. About 28 percent of the people work in agriculture, 25 percent in industry, and the remaining are employed in services. This includes work in businesses such as stores, banks, schools, and trade.

Opposite: **Iran is the world's leading pistachio producer.**

Rural women thresh wheat with sticks.

A tanker takes on oil at Kharg Island.

About 15 percent of the Iranian workforce is without a job. Unemployment is a major concern for Iran because nearly two-thirds of the population is under thirty years old. As more and more young people enter the labor force, many more jobs will need to be created or the unemployment rate will only increase.

The Oil Industry

Iran is the second-largest crude oil exporter in the Middle East, trailing only Saudi Arabia. Oil is Iran's leading industry, accounting for about 80 percent of the country's exports. The strength of Iran's economy is closely tied to the oil industry. In general, when oil prices are high, life is good. When oil prices fall, the economy falls along with it.

Money Facts

The basic unit of currency in Iran is the rial. Ten rials equal 1 toman. Coins are issued with values of 10, 50, 100, and 250 rials. Paper money comes in values of 100, 200, 500, 1,000, 2,000, 5,000, 10,000, and 50,000 rials. Most bills show Ayatollah Khomeini on the front. On the back are images of Iranian cities, landscapes, or sites important to Islam. In 2007, US$1 was worth more than 9,000 rials.

Many countries around the world need to buy oil for their own economies to thrive. In recent years, world demand for oil has increased, in part because of the booming economies of China and India. This has been good for Iran.

Since 1979, the Iranian oil industry has been completely nationalized. The government owns and runs it. During the 1979 hostage crisis, the United States applied economic sanctions to Iran. The United States refused to buy Iranian products or invest in the country. It convinced some other nations and organizations to do the same. With only limited outside help, the Iranian oil industry has developed more slowly than it would have otherwise.

Iran is the world's fourth-largest oil exporter. It exports about 60 percent of the oil it produces.

Weights and Measures

Iran uses the metric system. In this system, the basic unit of weight is the kilogram, which equals 2.2 pounds. The basic unit of length is the meter, which equals 3.3 feet.

Iran cannot expand its oil industry without foreign help. It does not have the money or the technical expertise to modernize its outdated equipment. Today, Iran exports less oil than it did in the 1970s, although its oil income has not fallen because of the huge rise in oil prices in recent years.

Ironically, Iran imports gasoline because it does not have enough refineries that turn the crude oil into gasoline. In fact, Iran is the world's second-largest importer of gas after the United States. The Iranian government subsidizes, or helps pay for, the gas before it reaches consumers. This makes it very cheap. Though this may sound good in the short run, it puts a major strain on the government's budget. It also means demand for gas is high. Consumption of gas in Iran has increased 50 percent in recent years.

What Iran Grows, Makes, and Mines	
Agriculture (2005)	
Wheat	14,500,000 metric tons
Sugar beets	5,273,000 metric tons
Sugarcane	4,723,000 metric tons
Manufacturing	
Cement (2000)	23,300,000 metric tons
Steel (2002)	7,300,000 metric tons
Sugar (1998)	863,000 metric tons
Mining	
Crude oil (2005)	3,979,000 barrels per day
Natural gas (2004)	83,900,000,000 cubic meters
Iron (2000)	10,776,000 metric tons

Manufacturing

A wide variety of products are made in Iran. Automobile production leads the manufacturing sector. In 2005, Iran's auto manufacturers, Khodro and Saipa, made more than a million new cars. The country also makes appliances, telecommunications equipment, processed foods, medicines, carpets, and leather products. Steel production is playing an increasingly large role in Iran's economy.

The Art of Making Carpets

The carpets made in Iran are renowned as the world's best. They are often considered works of art and may be seen just as often hanging from walls as spread on floors.

Iranians have more than two thousand years of expertise in making carpets. In the seventeenth century, Iranians bred sheep with especially fine wool and grew color-rich plants to use as natural dyes. The best carpets then and now are handmade. Today, however, many are made by machine.

The city of Isfahan is the center of Iranian carpet production, but each province in the country takes pride in making its own unique carpets. For example, carpets from Kirman are made from locally grown cotton and are famously soft and colorful. Carpets made in Qum are made from goat's wool and are decorated with bird and flower designs.

A carpet's price is determined by quality, workmanship, and design. One way to determine quality is the number of knots in the carpet. The more knots, the more expensive the carpet.

Agriculture

Iran is so dry that only about 10 percent of the land can be used for farming. Many fields must be irrigated for crops to grow. Rice is an important part of the Iranian diet, but it requires a lot of water. The main rice fields are located in the wet Caspian lowlands, which get the most rainfall of anywhere in the country. Yet even there, the rice fields need irrigation.

Iranian farmers also grow wheat, barley, sugar beets, sugar-cane, and potatoes. Much of the wheat is used to make bread. Barley is mainly used to feed animals.

Nuts are an important part of Iranian agriculture. Iran is especially famous for its sweet-tasting pistachios. Many tra-

Rice plants are often grown in fields submerged in water. Rice is a staple of the Iranian diet.

ditional desserts are made from these nuts. Walnuts and almonds are also grown in Iran.

Fruit trees grow in various parts of the country. Dates and bananas grow along the Persian Gulf, and the Caspian region produces citrus fruit. Apples, pears, peaches, grapes, and cherries are grown in the central plateau, and many types of melons are grown throughout the country.

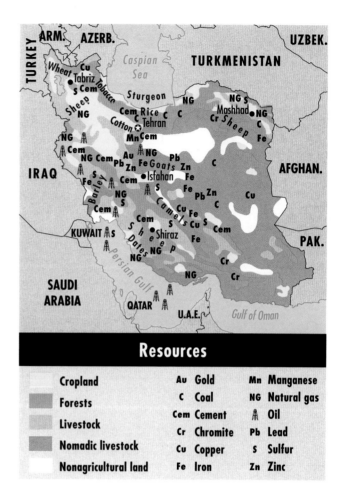

Resources

☐ Cropland	**Au** Gold	**Mn** Manganese
▨ Forests	**C** Coal	**NG** Natural gas
▦ Livestock	**Cem** Cement	🛢 Oil
▩ Nomadic livestock	**Cr** Chromite	**Pb** Lead
☐ Nonagricultural land	**Cu** Copper	**S** Sulfur
	Fe Iron	**Zn** Zinc

Livestock and Fish

Many rural Iranians raise sheep, goats, cattle, and chickens. They do not raise enough to feed the entire country, however, so most meat is imported. But the country is self-sufficient in fish. The Caspian Sea and the Persian Gulf are the country's two largest fishing areas. The Persian Gulf provides sardines, tuna, snapper, swordfish, and shrimp, while sturgeon, white salmon, pike, and catfish are caught in the Caspian Sea.

Caspian sturgeon produce fish eggs that are sold as caviar. Iranian caviar is rare and expensive. Most of it is exported to Russia and western Europe. Pollution has caused Caspian sturgeon to become endangered, however, so this industry's future is uncertain.

All newspapers in Iran are subject to government censorship.

Government Services

The government owns many businesses in Iran, so it is a major employer. Teachers, doctors, and oil-industry workers are all government employees. The government gives many contracts to nonprofit organizations called *bonyads*.

The bonyads, which are run by clerics, do not pay taxes. It is estimated that bonyads such as the Foundation for the Oppressed, the Martyrs Foundation, and War Wounded collectively own more than US$100 billion in assets and control more than 40 percent of the non-oil sector of the Iranian economy. Bonyads dominate the import and export businesses. Businesspeople who do not work for bonyads suffer because they do not get the same tax break. This makes it difficult for independent businesses to compete and make a profit.

Communications

The government owns or controls much of the media in Iran including newspapers, radio stations, and television stations. Anything that is printed or broadcast is subject to government censorship. If people distribute information that is considered un-Islamic, they can be fined or imprisoned.

The Iranian government may control its domestic media, but it cannot control the international media. Still, it tries to limit people's access to it. For example, the government tries to control which Internet sites can be viewed. But young people have increasingly found ways to get around the government blocks. Iran has many Internet cafés, where people can access news and information from the outside world. The Internet also enables Iranians to share their stories and information with the world community.

Young women use the Internet at a coffee shop in Tehran.

Satellite dishes, which enable people to watch television shows from around the world, are illegal in Iran. They are also increasingly common. Though the police are allowed to confiscate satellite dishes, they cannot keep up. They take one down, and another sprouts up in days.

Cell phone use is also on the rise in Iran. The number of cell phone users doubled between 2006 and 2007. At this rate, the number of cell phones in Iran will soon pass the number of landlines. The state-owned Telecommunications Company of Iran dominates the cell phone market. Iran also makes and exports cell phones.

Beaming TV to Iran

Iran's satellite dishes capture television signals from many places around the world. The United States is among those countries that beam signals toward Iran. About six hundred thousand Iranians live in Los Angeles, California. Some of them make TV programs that are directed to Iran. The Iranian residents of Los Angeles have nicknamed the city Tehrangeles, a combination of Tehran and Los Angeles. Among the more popular programs in Iran is the Oprah Winfrey show.

A Diverse Nation

To say you are an Iranian is like saying you are an American or a Canadian. It identifies your nationality but not your ethnic group. Iran is home to many different ethnic groups, each with its own distinct identity. Some have long roots in the region. Others are more recent arrivals.

Opposite: **About 23 percent of Iranians are under fifteen years old.**

Persians

About 51 percent of Iranians are Persians. They are the descendants of the Elamites and Aryans who arrived in the region thousands of years ago. Persians have had the most profound influence on the country, but non-Persians have added their own color to the tapestry that is Iran.

Slightly more than half of Iranians are Persians. They are the dominant group in the city of Tehran.

Iran's Ethnic Groups

Persians	51%
Azeris	24%
Gilakis and Mazandaranis	8%
Kurds	7%
Arabs	3%
Baluchis	2%
Luris	2%
Turkmen	2%
Other	1%

Many Kurds live along the Iran-Turkey border.

The Azeris

The Azeris are the largest minority ethnic group in Iran, making up about 24 percent of the population. In Iran, they are commonly referred to as Turks. Most live in the northwest part of the country, in a region called Azerbaijan, which is on the border with Turkey and the Republic of Azerbaijan. The Azeris speak a language called Azeri. It is a Turkic language blended with Persian.

Most Azeris are Shi'i Muslims. Many make a living by herding livestock and farming. Others work as merchants in bazaars throughout Iran. Many Azeris are also active in politics and the clergy. Azeri men tend to wear traditional goats'-wool hats. Azeri music and dancing are well integrated into Iranian culture.

The Gilaki and Mazandarani

The Gilaki and the Mazandarani peoples live in northern Iran near the Caspian Sea. The Gilaki and the Mazandarani speak Persian along with local dialects. Most Gilaki and Mazandarani fish or farm. Their strong and distinctive cooking traditions have spread across Iran. In particular, their seafood dishes have become popular throughout the country. The Gilaki and the Mazandarani are generally less religious than Persians.

Kurds

About 7 percent of the people in Iran are Kurds. The Kurds, who are descended from the ancient Medes, have long lived in Iran. They speak their own language, Kurdish, which is related to Persian. Kurds also live in Iraq, Turkey, and Syria. Some Kurds have tried to carve out an independent nation, but they have not yet succeeded.

Traditional Kurdish women wear long, bright dresses.

Iran's Ethnic Groups

- ■ Arabs
- ■ Azeris
- ■ Baluchis
- ■ Gilakis
- ■ Kurds
- □ Luris
- ■ Mazandaranis
- ■ Persians
- ■ Qashqais
- ■ Talyshi
- ■ Turkmen
- ■ Other

□ Sparsely populated area

Most Kurds are Sunni Muslims, and many practice a mystical form of Islam called Sufism. They wear traditional clothing. The men dress in short jackets and baggy pants. The women wear colorful dresses over baggy pants.

Other Ethnic Groups

Iran is also home to many smaller ethnic groups. Arabs make up about 3 percent of the population. They live mostly near the border with Iraq, along the Persian Gulf coast, and on the islands in the Gulf. They speak a dialect of Arabic. Arab Iranians tend to have darker skin than other Iranians. Many work in the oil industry. Those who live along the coastal regions are Sunni, whereas those near the Iraq border are Shi'i. Arab women wear ankle bracelets that jingle when they walk, and some have tattoos on their faces. Men generally wear a long, white, sleeveless tunic and a turban.

Turkmen are descended from the Turkish tribes that once ruled Iran. Today, they live in the northeast of the country. Turkmen speak their own language. They are Sunni Muslims, and some also practice Sufism. The women dress in bright colors and wear distinctive floral shawls. Men tuck their trousers into their boots and wear large sheepskin hats.

Wrestling and horseracing are central to the culture of the Turkmen. Both of these sports are part of religious celebrations and weddings. Turkmen are known throughout Iran as excellent horse breeders.

Most Luris live in western Iran. They speak Luri, a dialect of Old Persian. They make up about 2 percent of the population. The Baluchis, who make up another 2 percent of the population, live in dry, barren southeastern Iran. They are part of a nomadic tribe that has spread into Pakistan and Afghanistan. The Baluchis, who are Sunni Muslims, speak their own language, Baluchi. They are especially famous for their camel races.

Iran is also home to some Armenians, who live mostly in Tehran, Isfahan, and Tabriz. A few Assyrians live in the northwest. Both

An elderly Baluchi woman near the Pakistan border. Pakistan has the largest Baluchi population, followed by Iran.

Armenians and Assyrians are Christians, a small minority in Muslim-dominated Iran. Christians have their own churches and are allowed to practice their religion.

Refugees

An estimated two million refugees live in Iran. Most are from Afghanistan. Some fled war, others famine. After terrorists attacked the United States on September 11, 2001,

Armenian women stand in front of a church in Tehran. Though they are not Muslim, they must still cover their hair.

the United States responded by bombing Afghanistan. Afghans streamed across the border into Iran to escape the American bombing. The Iranian government has tried to send them back, but they have had little success.

Many Kurdish refugees have also entered Iran. They fled Iraq and Turkey, where they faced persecution.

Afghans at a refugee processing center near Tehran. About 5 percent of the Afghans in Iran live in refugee camps, while the rest live and work in cities around the country.

Nomadic Tribes

Iran is home to approximately ninety-six nomadic tribes. These tribes are divided into hundreds of different clans. Because they move about, nomads are difficult to count. But officials estimate that there are more than a million nomadic people in Iran. The nomadic tribes are well organized. They have clear customs, social organization, and tribal administration. Tribes have their own territories. Many of Iran's ethnic groups have nomadic tribes within their populations, including Turkmen, Persians, Kurds, Luris, Arabs, and Baluchis.

The largest nomadic tribes are the Chaharmahal and the Bakhtiyari, who live in east-central Iran. These tribes live in goat-hair tents while they graze their animals. When they are ready to leave, they pull up stakes and move on to other pasturelands.

A teacher talks to a student at a girls' school in Tehran. Almost 23 percent of Iran's government spending goes to education.

Education

Until the 1940s, few Iranian children went to school. At the time, only about 10 percent of Iranians could read and write. The nation has put great effort into improving its literacy rate in recent decades. By 2004, 84 percent of men and 70 percent of women were literate.

Most Iranian children begin school at age six. They are required to attend school for eight years. High school is optional. Throughout primary school, middle school, and high school, boys and girls are taught in separate classes.

Getting into college is difficult. Many more high school students want to go to college than there are spaces for them. Students are admitted based on their scores on a national entrance exam. The number of women admitted to universities has risen steadily in recent years. More than half of Iranian college students are women.

Education is free all the way from primary school through college. Iran also has many private colleges and universities. Students must pay to attend these.

Common Persian Words and Phrases

bale	yes
na	no
salam	hello
madar	mother
pedar	father
khoda hafez	good-bye
Hal-e shuma chetur-e?	How are you?
motashakkeram	thank you
Khahesh mikonam.	You are welcome.
lotfan	please

Students enjoy a discussion at a university in Tehran.

Population of Major Cities

Tehran	14,000,000
Mashhad	2,000,000
Tabriz	1,700,000
Isfahan	1,000,000
Shiraz	850,000

Persian is written in Arabic script, which has no capital letters.

Speaking Persian

The official language in Iran is Persian. (In the Persian language, it is called *Farsi*.) Many Persian words come directly from Arabic, but Persian is not related to Arabic. Instead, it is an Indo-European language, a member of the same language family as English, Hindi, Russian, and Spanish. Many Persian words have made their way into English. They include *bazaar*, *caravan*, *khaki*, *lime*, *magic*, *pajamas*, *paradise*, *spinach*, *tiger*, and *tulip*.

Persian is written using the Arabic alphabet. Arabic script reads from right to left, the opposite direction of the script used to write English. Arabic writing can be quite beautiful. The elegant, flowing script is often used in art. It appears in paintings, on pottery, and on mosaic tiles.

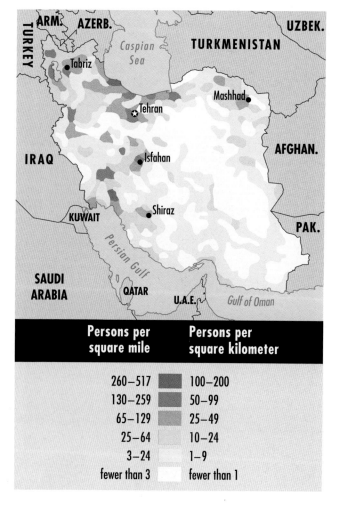

Persons per square mile		Persons per square kilometer
260–517		100–200
130–259		50–99
65–129		25–49
25–64		10–24
3–24		1–9
fewer than 3		fewer than 1

City Life, City Problems

Iran's population is nearly seventy million, and it is still rising. In recent decades, more and more Iranians have left the countryside and moved into cities. Today, more than half of Iranians live in urban areas. Iran's cities have difficulty keeping up with the population growth. The rising population strains what were already poor sewage and water systems. This poses health risks, as does air pollution.

Tehran, in particular, has horrible pollution. Schools in Tehran occasionally close because of high levels of air pollution. Efforts are being made to ease the problem. New cars must now have air pollution controls. But the older cars have no pollution controls at all, so any improvement in air quality will likely take a long time.

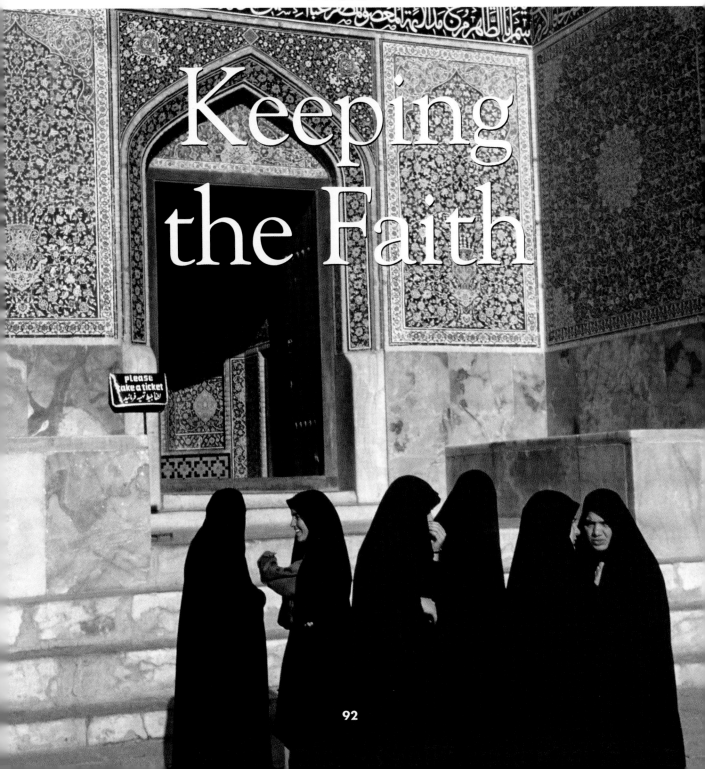

Keeping the Faith

please
take a ticket

Some young women in Iran dress fashionably, though they always wear a head scarf and keep their arms and legs covered.

WHEN IRAN BECAME AN ISLAMIC REPUBLIC IN 1979, Islam became more than a religion—its moral code became a way of life. That moral code applies not only to Muslims. It applies to everyone, regardless of his or her religious beliefs.

How does Islam affect the daily life of Iranians? The most obvious example is that all women and girls must cover their heads, arms, and legs in keeping with Islam's requirement that women dress modestly. Some young Iranian women, however, wear their head scarves farther back on their heads, allowing their hair to show. In this small, and some would say rebellious, act, they show that there is more than one way to interpret the rules of Islam.

Opposite: **Women gather outside the Sheikh Lotf Allah Mosque in Isfahan.**

Muhammad and the Birth of Islam

Like Christianity and Judaism, Islam is a monotheistic religion: its believers worship one god. A follower of Islam is called a Muslim, which means "he who submits to the will of God." The Arabic word for God is *Allah*.

The story of Islam begins with the Prophet Muhammad. Muhammad was born in A.D. 570 in the city of Mecca, on the Arabian Peninsula. Muslims believe that in 610, Muhammad began having visions of an angel, Gabriel. This angel told him that he, Muhammad, was the messenger of God and that it was his responsibility to spread the word of God.

Muhammad received many revelations through the angel Gabriel. He started preaching God's messages.

Muslims pray at the Grand Mosque in Mecca. Mecca is the holiest city in Islam.

As time went on, Muhammad became more and more popular. The rulers of Mecca became concerned about his growing influence. They began attacking the newly converted Muslims. In 622, Muhammad and his followers migrated to

Medina, another city on the Arabian Peninsula, where they found a more welcoming environment. That year became the first year in the Muslim calendar.

Muhammad eventually returned to Mecca and conquered it. Mecca became the headquarters for Islam. Muhammad's return to Mecca is the foundation of a pilgrimage that Muslims still do today. It is one of the Five Pillars of Islam. All Muslims are required to follow these principles.

The Five Pillars of Islam

All Muslims are expected to follow five practices called the Five Pillars of Islam. They are:

1. Making the declaration that there is no god but God, and that Muhammad is the messenger of God.

2. Praying daily. Sunni Muslims pray five times a day, and Shi'i Muslims pray three times a day. Muslims pray wherever they are—at work, at school, at home, or at a mosque, a Muslim house of worship.

3. Giving to the poor.

4. Fasting during the holy month of Ramadan. Muslims must not eat or drink from sunrise to sunset during this month. Pregnant women, the old, and the sick do not have to follow this rule.

5. Making a pilgrimage to Mecca (left) at least once in their lifetime if they are physically and financially able.

Muslims believe that Muhammad is the last in a line of prophets, God's messengers, who include Noah, Abraham, Moses, and Jesus. When the angel Gabriel appeared to Muhammad, he explained how people should behave. For example, they should not collect interest when they lend others money. They should help the poor. Above all, Muslims believe that there is only one true god.

Shi'i and Sunni

Just as Christianity has different branches, there are different sects of Islam. The two most prominent are Shi'i and Sunni. Worldwide, the Sunnis are by far the largest group, accounting for about 85 percent of the more than one billion Muslims on the planet. In Iran, however, Shi'is dominate, making up about 80 percent of the population.

The Qur'an

The holy book of Islam is called the Qur'an. Muslims believe that God dictated the Qur'an to Muhammad. To Muslims, the Qur'an is the ultimate authority on legal and religious matters.

The split between these two groups dates back to the earliest days of Islam. When Muhammad died in 632, he did not appoint anyone to take over as leader of his movement. Disagreements arose over who should become the caliph, Muhammad's successor. The two leading contenders were Abu Bakr, the father of Muhammad's second wife, and Ali, Muhammad's cousin and son-in-law. In time, Abu Bakr became the first caliph. Ali became the fourth caliph.

Ali's supporters continued to believe that he was the legitimate successor of Muhammad. They were called *Shi'at 'Ali* ("followers of Ali"). Today, they are known as Shi'is. They believe that the true leader of Islam should be a direct descendant of Muhammad. Sunnis accept the authority of the caliphs who succeeded Muhammad over the centuries.

Sunnis and Shi'is practice Islam in slightly different ways. For example, Shi'is believe that religious doctrine can be

Fatimah Is Fatimah

In the 1970s, 'Ali Shariati, an author and sociologist, wrote a book called *Fatimah Is Fatimah*. In it, he portrayed Muhammad's daughter as a social activist who helped the poor. The book inspired many women to return to their cultural heritage at a time when the westernization promoted by the shah of Iran was seen as un-Islamic.

The book inspired some women to revert to wearing the traditional dress of Iran. It consists of a head scarf, a long coat, and trousers.

reinterpreted throughout history, while Sunnis do not. The rules governing divorce and inheritance are more favorable to women in Shi'i Islam than in Sunni Islam.

Neither Sunni nor Shi'i Muslims have a formal priesthood, although Shi'is have something more like it. The most obvious difference today between Sunni and Shi'i Islam is that Shi'i religious leaders are both powerful and independent of government control. This was what made the Islamic Revolution possible in Iran. It is also most likely why the revolution has not been repeated elsewhere. Since the early nineteenth century, the Sunni clergy have basically been government appointees. This means they are far less likely to challenge the authority and power of the government, which is exactly what Ayatollah Khomeini's followers did in 1979.

Religious Holidays

Ramadan is the ninth month of the Islamic calendar. Throughout this month, Muslims do not eat or drink from sunrise to sundown. They believe that fasting helps improve a person's spiritual life. It helps a person be more compassionate toward poor people, and it cleanses the body.

Muslims celebrate the end of Ramadan with a three-day festival called 'Id al-Fitr. During this holiday, people visit family and friends and give gifts. It is similar in spirit to Christmas. Special foods such as lamb stuffed with dried fruit are prepared. Candies and delicious sweet pastries are also part of the celebration.

'Id al-Adha, the Festival of the Sacrifice, celebrates the completion of the pilgrimage to Mecca. The celebration begins during the last month of the Islamic calendar and lasts three days.

On Ashura, many Shi'i Muslims take part in mournful processions to commemorate the martyrdom of Muhammad's grandson Husayn.

Religious Minorities

While the vast majority of Iranians are Shi'i Muslims, some Iranians do follow other religions. Baha'is, Jews, Christians, and Zoroastrians combine to make up about 1 percent of the population. All but the Baha'is are recognized religious minorities in Iran. They have government representation and can openly practice their faith.

The Baha'i religion is a reform movement founded in the nineteenth century within Islam by Mirza 'Ali Muhammad. He was called the *Bab*, a title that comes from the word for "gate." Baha'is believe that the Bab

Religions in Iran

Islam	99.0%
Baha'i	0.6%
Christianity	0.3%
Judaism	0.07%
Zoroastrianism	0.03%

About twenty-five thousand Jews live in Iran.

was a messenger of God, just like Moses, Jesus, and Muhammad. The Islamic clergy felt threatened by him and believed his teachings to be anti-Islamic. He was executed in 1850. His follower Mirza Husain 'Ali, who was called Baha'ullah ("the Glory of God"), was responsible for spreading the Baha'i religion. Baha'is are sometimes critical of Islamic teachings. They consider some Muslim practices discriminatory, especially those that apply to women. The Baha'i religion is illegal in Iran, but about 350,000 Baha'is continue to make the country their home.

Jews have lived in Iran for about 2,500 years, although many left after the 1979 revolution. Most of those who remain live in Iran's larger cities. Many work as merchants or in the jewelry business.

Most Sunni Muslims in Iran are Kurds, Baluchis, or Turkmen. They live along the borders of Iran. Most Christians in Iran are Armenians or Assyrians. Armenians live mostly in the cities of Tehran, Isfahan, and Tabriz. The Armenian cathedral of Saint Savior is in Isfahan, where there is a large Armenian community. The Armenians maintain their own culture, speak the Armenian language, and are allowed to attend Sunday church services.

A Zoroastrian fire temple in Yadz. Yadz Province in central Iran is home to the largest number of Zoroastrians in the country.

Another religion practiced in Iran is Zoroastrianism. It was founded by a philosopher named Zoroaster, who was born around 600 B.C. Zoroastrians believe in a supreme being called Ahura Mazda. They also believe that life is a battle between good and evil. At the end of life, people are judged on how well they fought this battle.

The Sufis

Sufism is an Islamic tradition focused on the spiritual and mystical aspects of the religion. The term *Sufi* comes from the Arabic word *suf*, meaning "wool." This is a reference to the rough cloaks Sufis traditionally wore. Sufis believe that a personal experience with God can best be achieved through prayer, meditation, and self-discipline. The Sufis have no mosques or temples. Their philosophy is to live in the world but not be of the world. This means that they try to live simply and dedicate their lives to good works.

The best-known Sufi is a poet named Jalal al-Din al-Rumi (1207–1273), who was born in northeastern Persia in an area that is now a part of Afghanistan. He is famous throughout the world for his mystical writings. A grand shrine (left) rises above his tomb in Konya, Turkey.

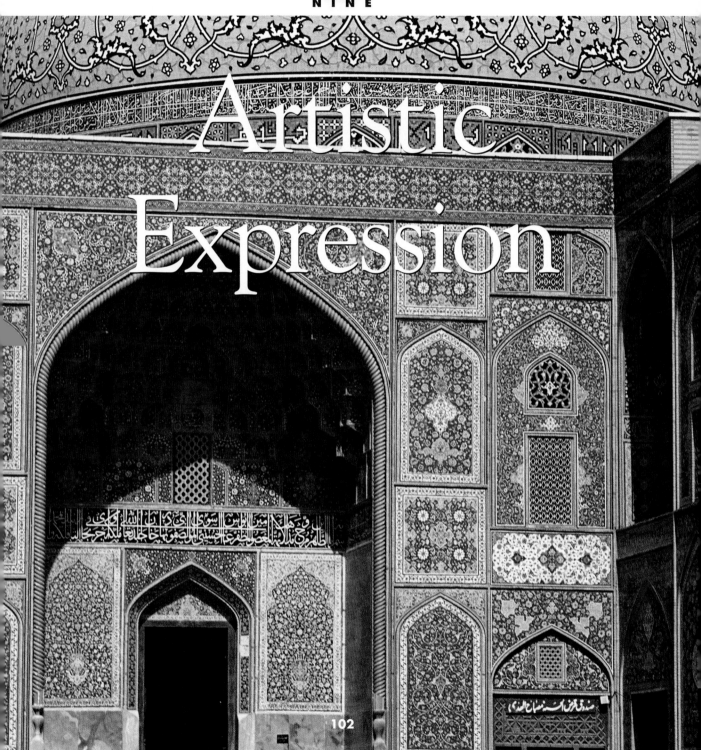

Artistic Expression

Some of the earliest examples of Iranian art are ancient pieces of pottery decorated with animal figures. As Iranian culture developed, so did its distinctive art forms. Intricate metalwork reached its peak during the Sasanian era (A.D. 224–642), and the Persian art of painting in miniature dates back to the Seljuk dynasty (1037–1187). Through the centuries, painters, weavers, poets, and calligraphers have contributed to Iran's amazing treasure trove of art.

Opposite: **Iranian mosques are noted for their open vaulted halls.**

Many mosques are decorated with elaborate tile work.

Architecture

Mosques throughout the Muslim world are modeled on Iranian styles. Their design is actually quite simple. It features a dome and vaulted halls extending toward a central courtyard. It is the tiles that cover the buildings that make them exceptionally beautiful.

Elaborate tile making flourished under the Safavid dynasty (1501–1722). Most of the tiles are blue, but yellow, white, olive green, and browns are also used. The Safavid period is considered the golden age of Iranian architecture. The domes of this period are notable for their height

and beautiful form. The most elegant examples of Safavid architecture are in Isfahan. In particular, the Sheikh Lotf Allah Mosque and the Friday Mosque are considered world treasures. Their geometric and floral patterns show off the exceptional skills of the artists who made them. Isfahan's Chahal Sutun Building and 'Ali Qapu Palace also showcase the extraordinary architecture of the Safavid era.

Architecture clearly has a functional purpose—people live, work, study, and pray in buildings. Buildings also reflect the culture of a place and time. In the 1940s, Iran was quickly

Sheikh Loft Allah Mosque in Isfahan is one of the most celebrated mosques in Iran. It is famed for its elaborate mosaics.

A Call to Prayer

Tall, narrow towers called minarets rise above mosques. Traditionally, a person called a muezzin climbed to a balcony near the top of a minaret and announced when it was time for Muslims to pray.

These days, many muezzins do not have to climb to the top of a minaret to issue the call to prayer. Instead, they make the announcement using a microphone and loudspeakers.

becoming more westernized. By the late 1960s, Iranian architects wanted to preserve elements of traditional styles so they would not get lost during this time of rapid change. They wanted to adapt to the times without becoming pure imitators of the West. This resulted in buildings such as the

The Azadi Tower was completed in 1971.

Azadi Tower, which was built in Tehran to celebrate the 2,500th anniversary of the Persian Empire. The building looks like an upside-down letter Y. It incorporates Sasanian and Islamic styles of architecture yet also looks completely modern.

Expressions of this blending of old and new styles can also be seen in such buildings as the Tehran Museum of Contemporary Art and the Tehran University College of Social Sciences, which recalls the famed palace of Persepolis.

A weaver repairs the edge of a carpet. Persian carpets have long been prized around the world.

Persian Carpets

Carpet making is another classic Iranian art form. Many people consider Persian carpets the best in the world. Traditionally, floral patterns, geometric shapes, and, eventually, verses from the Qur'an were woven into the carpets. The finest Persian carpets come from the eighteenth century. Today, these carpets hang in museums.

Iranians use carpets to cover floors and to decorate walls. Nomads often use carpets as tent doors. Muslims also use carpets during prayers. Prayer carpets are generally small, so people can simply roll them out and kneel on them.

The World's Largest Prayer Carpet

Workers at the Iran Carpet Company spent four years weaving what is believed to be the world's largest prayer carpet. Named the Carpet of Wonder, it is 5,194 square yards (4,343 sq m) and has 1.7 billion knots. The carpet covers the floor of a prayer hall in the Grand Mosque in Muscat, Oman.

Life in Small Detail

One of the most notable miniaturists of the fifteenth century was Kamal al-Din Bihzad. He was famous for his geometric style. Bihzad led a workshop where artists illustrated books in his style. The rich words of poets, in particular, inspired Bihzad to portray people and daily life in detail.

Visual Arts

Painting, photography, and other visual arts are well represented in art galleries and museums throughout Iran. Artists today still practice an age-old form of painting called miniature. This tradition dates to the 1500s. Miniatures, as the name implies, are quite small. As time went on, they became more and more detailed, showing vivid court scenes and hunting expeditions. Traditional miniatures were usually book illustrations.

A miniature illustrates the work of Nezami, a great epic poet of the 1100s.

Another ancient yet living Iranian art form is calligraphy. Calligraphers write letters and words so beautifully that they are considered art. Calligraphy is used to adorn everything from buildings to vases. Verses from the Qur'an and the Prophet Muhammad decorate mosques throughout the country. In the sixteenth century, Iranian calligraphers were considered the best in the Islamic world.

Thousands of years ago, ancient people in what is now Iran painted images of animals and hunting scenes on cave walls. Artists today decorate walls in subway stations. Many of the colorful murals in Tehran's subway stations incorporate enameled tile, pottery, and metalwork.

Iranians have long used metal to produce art. They make beautiful copper bowls and trays decorated with calligraphy. These functional works of art are sold in bazaars around the country.

Among the most famous modern Iranian artists is Sayyed 'Ali Akhbar Sanati. He studied with both miniaturists and sculptors. Sanati helped launch the first public museum in Tehran in 1945. Computers are also widely used to create art in Iran. The award-winning graphic art of Reza Abedini appears in magazine, posters, and museums.

Elaborate teapots called samovars sit in the window of a shop in Isfahan.

The Story of a Childhood

Persepolis: The Story of a Childhood is a graphic novel by a woman named Marjane Satrapi. Though it is written in the form of a comic book, it is not about superheroes. Instead, it tells the story of Satrapi's life as a young girl growing up during the Islamic Revolution. Satrapi was ten years old at the time, and the book describes the changes in Iran from a young girl's perspective. Satrapi talks about going to school with boys before the revolution. A year later, she had to go to a school with only girls. She also had to start wearing a head scarf. She and her schoolmates played with their scarves, using them as jump ropes. Of course, the teachers were not amused.

Eventually, Satrapi's parents sent her to Vienna, Austria, to finish her studies, because life in Iran had become increasingly difficult and dangerous for such an outspoken young woman. Today, Satrapi lives and works in Paris, France.

Inspiring Words

Poetry also has a long history in Iran. The shahs hired poets to entertain at their courts. Poetry remains a vital part of Iran's cultural life. Visual artists find inspiration in poetry, and many Iranians learn long poems by heart.

An early poet, Hakim Abulqasim Ferdosi, wrote epic poems documenting Persian history. Ferdosi was born in about 940. His most famous work is the *Shahnamah* (*Book of Kings*), which took him thirty years to complete. He wrote the poem in Persian at a time when Arabs controlled Iran. Ferdosi's epic helped preserve ancient Iranian culture and history.

Another great poet, Omar Khayyam, was born around 1047. His most famous work is the *Rubaiyat*. In the 1850s, a

Hafiz

A *hafiz* is someone who can recite the Qur'an from memory. Hafiz is also the nickname of an extraordinary poet named Khwaja Shams-ed-Din Muhammad. Hafiz was born in Shiraz in 1324. He eventually became a court poet, a teacher, and a Sufi master.

Today, Hafiz's books are as popular in Iran as the Qur'an—some people would say more so. Iranians use his poems as a guide for daily living. They randomly turn to a page and let the poem inspire their day.

Though Hafiz died hundreds of years ago, pilgrimages to his tomb (right) in Shiraz are a daily occurrence. His tomb is in a garden with a teahouse and a bookshop.

English poet Edward FitzGerald is best known for translating Omar Khayyam's *Rubaiyat*.

translation by an Englishman named Edward FitzGerald made Khayyam famous in the West. In Iran, he is also respected as a mathematician, historian, and astronomer.

Among the most celebrated modern poets was Ahmad Shamlu (1925–2000). Shamlu used simple imagery in his complex poems. He taught Persian literature in Tehran and wrote extensively on the poetry of Hafiz, one of Iran's most influential poets. Shamlu also spent a few months in prison for his political activism. In addition to writing poetry, Shamlu wrote film scripts and newspaper articles.

Film

Iranians have been making films since the early 1900s. Today, the Iranian film industry churns out tons of action movies, but the country is more famous for its serious films. Several current Iranian filmmakers have worldwide reputations.

The Iranian government censors the subject matter of films. Because of this, many Iranian movies focus on simple aspects of life rather than directly on political issues. For example, in the film *Children of Heaven*, a boy loses his sister's shoes, so he must share his own sneakers with her. Like many Iranian films, *Children of Heaven* used nonprofessional actors.

Many Iranian films tackle serious subjects. In her award-winning film *The Day I Became a Woman*, director Marzieh Meshkini explores what it means to be female in her native Iran. The first part of the film tells the story of a girl who turns

In 2004, Marzieh Meshkini released a film called *Stray Dogs*. It follows the lives of street children in war-torn Afghanistan.

nine years old. Because she is considered mature at that age, she must begin to wear a chador and is forbidden to play with her best friend, who is a boy. There are two versions of this film. Iranian censors required that some scenes be removed for the film to be shown in Iran. The complete version is available elsewhere in the world.

The Makhmalbaf Film Family

Mohsen Makhmalbaf was born in a poor neighborhood in Tehran in 1957. When he was seventeen, he was sent to prison for working against the shah. By the time he was released, the Islamic Revolution had taken place.

Makhmalbaf's early films celebrated Islamic values, but his later films questioned how they were being applied in Iran. Several of his films were banned because they were considered anti-Islamic. Today,

he is considered one of Iran's leading filmmakers. His films include *Gabbeh*, which concerns nomadic people whose carpets tell stories. Perhaps his most famous work is *Kandahar*, the story of a woman in Afghanistan stripped of her rights as a fundamentalist Islamic regime takes over.

Several members of Makhmalbaf's family are also filmmakers. His wife, Marzieh Meshkini, gained fame for *The Day I Became a Woman*. His daughter Samira (above) made a film called *Blackboards* when she was just twenty years old. It won an award at the famed Cannes Film Festival. Makhmalbaf's younger daughter, Hana, is also a filmmaker.

Music

Music has long been important to Iranian life. Classical Iranian music is played on instruments such as the *tar*, which has four strings, and the *oud*, which has nine to eleven strings. It also uses drums, tambourines, and wind instruments. Rhythms are simple and repetitive, and the tempo is generally fast. Poetry is often incorporated into classical Persian music. Shahram Nazeri is a popular classical Iranian musician who brings the work of Sufi poet Jalal al-Din al-Rumi to life.

The Islamic cultural authorities screen popular music and lyrics. But besides the music that is approved by the state, the country has an active underground rock music scene. The band O-Hum plays rock on Persian instruments and composes songs using the poetry of Hafiz. The group started as a garage band. They signed a recording contract, but their music was ultimately banned by the government. They put their music on the Internet instead of on a CD and allow people to download it for free.

Shahram Nazeri is one of the most respected singers in Iran. He is famous for his soulful performances.

Everyday Ways

114

NOTHING IS MORE IMPORTANT TO IRANIANS THAN family. Both men and women usually live with their families until they marry, and sometimes even after they marry. Families often gather to share picnics, go shopping, or make other group outings. Iranians spend a lot of time with their extended family, visiting aunts, uncles, cousins, and grandparents, as well as enjoying the company of their immediate family.

Iranians are generally considered warm and gracious people. Hospitality is an important part of Iranian culture. Iranians often entertain their guests by reading poetry aloud. They also offer endless cups of tea and delicious food. If you are a guest in an Iranian home, your plate will never be empty, and your glass will be refilled before you even finish it.

Opposite: **A Kurdish family poses in their home.**

Iranians traditionally eat sitting on the floor. The food is spread out on a carpet.

Iranian Manners

Being polite is important to Iranians, but their manners can be confusing to foreigners. For example, a person visiting someone's home should refuse an offer of food several times before accepting it. This allows the host to save face in the event that he or she does not have food ready to share. But generally, the host will insist that the visitor eat and drink. It may be taken as an insult if the visitor refuses the offer after the host has insisted three times.

Iranian courtesy also demands that hosts serve guests using their best plates. Iranians never sit with their back toward their elders. And they always ask guests about the health of their families and other loved ones.

Persian Cuisine

Iranian food is renowned for its distinctive and imaginative flavors. Iranian dishes include such interesting combinations as duck, pomegranates, and walnuts, or lamb, prunes, and cinnamon. Iranian seasonings are subtle but delectable. Rather than using a lot of garlic, for example, they use spices such

A wide variety of spices and other goods are available at markets in Iran.

as saffron, cinnamon, and cloves. Iranians also cook with lots of fresh herbs. Mint, dill, cilantro, and parsley are popular. These are mixed into rice dishes or eaten raw with meat dishes.

Rice dishes are the staple of the Iranian diet. Iranians frequently use fragrant basmati rice, often mixing it with lentils, raisins, dates, and nuts.

Popular meats include lamb, chicken, and fish. Pork is not eaten because Islam forbids it. Common vegetables include spinach, cauliflower, eggplant, and onions. Iranians frequently cook with fruits such as plums, apricots, and peaches. To balance the sweetness of the fruit, they frequently add sour flavors such as lemon, lime, and tangerine peel. Iranians serve yogurt and flat breads with most meals. They usually buy the bread at a bakery rather than making it at home.

When dining at home, Iranians serve guests from large platters of food. They usually put out far more food than the people at the table can eat. Their sense of hospitality calls for abundance. Many of the dishes are complicated. Some take hours to prepare. *Shirin polow*, for example, is a chicken and rice dish that requires soaking rice in warm water for two hours, slicing almonds and pistachios, boiling slivered orange peel, and sautéing chicken. The result is well worth the work, for it is a delicious and healthy meal.

Stews, kebabs, and soups are also on the menu at homes and in restaurants. A common drink is *dugh*, which is made with yogurt, soda water, mint, and ice. It is particularly refreshing on hot days.

Kebabs, a Signature Iranian Dish

Kebabs are chunks of meat threaded onto a skewer and grilled over charcoal. Meats used for kebabs include chicken, lamb, and combinations of ground meat. Kebabs are most often accompanied by mounds of rice and grilled tomatoes.

Iranians usually serve tea in glasses.

Tea is popular year-round, and the country is filled with teahouses. Many Iranians keep a samovar, or teapot, going all day long, just as some Americans have a pot of coffee at hand throughout the day. The tea is served in small glasses. Iranians do not put sugar into the tea. Instead, they place sugar cubes in their mouths and sip the tea through the cubes, allowing the sweetness to slowly dissolve.

Housing

Most Iranians live in cities. Urban Iranians usually live in apartment buildings. In the wealthy district of northern Tehran, the apartments are like those in any modern city around the world. They have central air-conditioning, indoor parking garages, and swimming pools. But that kind of home is the exception rather than the rule. Most Iranians' apartments are more modest.

An elderly nomadic woman sits in the shade of her tent. She is one of more than a million nomads in Iran.

Flowers and a pool grace the courtyard of a house in Julfa.

In smaller towns and in the countryside, homes are generally built around an enclosed courtyard, which has a garden and a small pool or fountain. Flower gardens are popular, and roses in particular are cherished. In rural areas, some homes are made from mud bricks. Many homes lack windows. Instead, the roof has vents to let air in.

Nomads have no permanent homes. Instead, they live in tents, which they can easily take down and carry from place to place.

Clothing

In Iran, most women wear head scarves and long, loose coats or chadors in public. But underneath these coverings, they often wear the latest European fashions or simple blue jeans.

Many Iranian boys dress much the same as young people in the West.

Nomadic women generally do not wear chadors. Instead, they wear colorful dresses and robes.

Some Iranian women color their nails and wear dramatic lipstick and eye makeup. Eyebrow shaping is taken to a high art form in Iran, and most women have their brows plucked to perfection.

Like Muslim women, Muslim men are expected to dress modestly. For most Iranian men, this means loose-fitting pants and shirts. Clerics wear black or brown robes. Those who are descendants of the Prophet Muhammad wear black turbans, while other Muslim scholars wear white turbans.

The Islamic Dress Code

The Qur'an says people should dress modestly, but it doesn't specifically say what clothing they should wear. The Islamic dress code has been interpreted in different ways in different countries.

In Iran, women are required by law to cover their heads and wear loose clothing, although the dress code has become much less oppressive in recent years.

While some Muslim women view the requirement as intrusive, others like it because it discourages others from judging them on their appearance or style of clothes.

Muslim men are also supposed to dress modestly, although what they wear is not strictly dictated by law, as it is for women.

Private and Public Life

Iranians, especially women, see themselves as having two distinct lives: *zaher*, public life, and *batin*, private life. Islamic law dictates how women dress and how they socialize in public. While this is also true for men, the rules are not the same. For example, women can work and hold public office, but they cannot be judges. In legal disputes, a woman's testimony is only worth half that of a man's.

Men and women are not allowed to socialize in public unless they are relatives or married. The police can ask couples to prove that they are married. Separate areas exist for men and women in public places. Women typically ride in the back of buses. Men and women do not swim together at the same beaches or ski on the same slopes.

Male and female students sit separately during a demonstration at Tehran University.

Many Iranians get married surrounded by flowers and other decorations.

Still, women have more freedom in Iran than in some other Muslim countries. They go to school, they drive, they own businesses, they work in many professions. Half the university students in Iran are women. Iranian women have been involved in protests against the government. Because women lack some freedoms, they are sometimes the ones pushing the most strongly for change and modernization.

Getting Married

Traditionally in Iran, marriage partners were chosen by a couple's parents. While this is still sometimes the case in rural Iran, today it is more common for couples to meet each other through friends and coworkers. Still, most Iranians seek the approval of their parents before they marry. Couples typically marry in their twenties, although the legal age at which a girl can marry is nine. Weddings can be lavish. The bill is typically paid by the groom's family. At most Iranian weddings, the bride wears white, and the groom wears a black or blue suit.

A distinctive element in a Persian wedding is the *sofreh aghd*, or "spread." The sofreh aghd is a group of items placed on a white cloth on the floor. The marriage ceremony takes place at the head of this spread. The spread is arranged so that the couple will face the light of the rising sun. Each item in the spread has a symbolic meaning. Common items on the sofreh aghd include a mirror to reflect light into the future, two candelabras for fire and energy, flat bread for prosperity, and decorated eggs for fertility. The sofreh aghd is not Islamic. Instead, it is distinctly Persian and can be traced back to the ancient Zoroastrian faith.

During the wedding ceremony, married friends hold a cloth over the couple's heads while two sugar cubes are rubbed above the couple to symbolically sweeten their union. The cleric (or other official if it is a non-Muslim wedding) asks the bride three times if she agrees to the marriage. She declines until the third time, when the groom's father offers money or something else of value. Then she agrees. An extravagant feast follows the wedding.

Most Iranian brides wear white gowns.

The Sporting Life

Wrestling and soccer are the two most popular sports in Iran. Iranian wrestlers dominate in world freestyle wresting. In the 2000 Olympics, Iranian wrestler 'Alireza Dabir won a gold medal. In 2006, Iranians won five of seven events in the World Cup freestyle wrestling competition.

Spectators flock to Azadi Sports Complex in Tehran to watch the national soccer team play. In 2006, women were allowed to attend matches for the first time since the Islamic Revolution. Several Iranian soccer stars play for top teams in Europe.

'Alireza Dabir is one of Iran's greatest wrestlers.

The House of Strength

A *zurkhaneh* is a traditional Iranian gymnasium. Its name means "house of strength." The exercises and activities done in a zurkhaneh date back thousands of years. Originally used for military training, they mix martial arts and spirituality.

In a zurkhaneh, a group of men gathers in a pit where they perform feats that test their strength and agility. The men lift wooden clubs. They stretch, bend, and twirl. All of this is done to the beat of drums. Epic poetry and religious songs add to the spiritual nature of the zurkhaneh.

Average Iranians take part in a wide variety of sports, from bowling to skiing to polo to camel racing. Adventure seekers trek through the mountains, scuba dive, and hang glide. Yoga classes are becoming increasingly popular, especially in the

Rahman Rezaei (left) is one of many Iranian soccer stars who plays in Europe. He plays for a team in Livorno, Italy.

Crowds gather in a garden to celebrate the end of Nawruz.

cities. Iranians of all ages enjoy walks through nature. Video games are popular among young people, who often play them in Internet cafés.

Celebrating the New Year

Iranians celebrate many holidays throughout the year. The largest and most joyful celebration is Nawruz, the Persian New Year. This thirteen-day celebration begins on March 21, the first day of spring, and is all about the renewal of life. In preparation for Nawruz, Iranians clean their homes thoroughly, throw away worn-out items, and buy new shoes and clothes. Many Iranians visit family and friends during Nawruz. Children especially love Nawruz because they often receive gifts from relatives.

Major Holidays

February 11	Victory of the Islamic Revolution
March 20	Oil Nationalization Day
March 21	Nawruz (Persian New Year)
April 1	Islamic Republic Day
June 4	Death of Ayatollah Khomeini
June 5	1963 Uprising

During Nawruz, Iranians set up a special table in their home where they place symbolic items, each beginning with the letter S in Persian. *Seeb* (apple) represents beauty. *Senjed* (dried lotus fruit) stands for love. *Sumac* (a spice) symbolizes new life. *Sabzeh* (wheat, barley, or lentil sprouts) symbolizes rebirth. *Samanu* (wheat-germ paste) stands for affluence. *Sir* (garlic) is for health. And *serkeh* (vinegar) symbolizes patience. Iranians also sprout wheat grass, which they will toss into a river on the thirteenth day of the new year. This is an ancient custom from the Zoroastrian religion.

Iranians believe that how they start the new year influences how their year will be. Therefore, Iranians celebrate with loved ones and forgive one another during this time. That way, they move into the new year, into the future, with joy.

The feast of Nawruz dates back to pre-Islamic times. Each item on the Nawruz table has symbolic meaning.

Timeline

Iranian History		World History
The Elamite civilization is established around the northern Persian Gulf.	3000 B.C.	
	2500 B.C.	Egyptians build the pyramids and the Sphinx in Giza.
The Aryans enter what is now Iran.	1500 B.C.	
Cyrus the Great becomes leader of the Achaemenid dynasty.	580 B.C.	
	563 B.C.	The Buddha is born in India.
Darius I expands the Persian Empire to its farthest reaches.	ca. 490 B.C.	
Alexander the Great conquers Persia.	330 B.C.	
The Sasanians establish the second Persian Empire.	A.D. 224	
	A.D. 313	The Roman emperor Constantine legalizes Christianity.
	610	The Prophet Muhammad begins preaching a new religion called Islam.
An Arab army enters Iran, bringing Islam to the region.	630s	
The Seljuks take over Iran.	1040	
	1054	The Eastern (Orthodox) and Western (Roman Catholic) Churches break apart.
	1095	The Crusades begin.
	1215	King John seals the Magna Carta.
The Mongols invade Iran.	1220	
	1300s	The Renaissance begins in Italy.
	1347	The plague sweeps through Europe.
	1453	Ottoman Turks capture Constantinople, conquering the Byzantine Empire.
	1492	Columbus arrives in North America.
	1500s	Reformers break away from the Catholic Church, and Protestantism is born.
The Safavid dynasty gains power in Iran.	1501	
Nadir Shah comes to power.	1736	
	1776	The U.S. Declaration of Independence is signed.

Iranian History

The Qajar dynasty is established.	1794
Great Britain and Russia vie for power in the region.	1800s
Iran's first constitution is written and its first legislature established.	1906
Oil is discovered; the Anglo-Persian Oil Company is established.	1908
Reza Shah Pahlavi becomes ruler.	1925
Reza Shah changes the country's name from Persia to Iran.	1935
The Trans-Iranian Railway linking the Persian Gulf and Caspian Sea is completed.	1939
Reza Shah abdicates in favor of his son Mohammad Reza.	1941
Iran nationalizes its oil industry.	1951
Forces loyal to Ayatollah Khomeini seize control of the country; the Islamic Republic of Iran is established; Iranian militants take hostages in the U.S. Embassy.	1979
The Iran-Iraq War.	1980–1988
Ayatollah Khomeini dies.	1989
Mahmoud Ahmadinejad is elected president.	2005

World History

1789	The French Revolution begins.
1865	The American Civil War ends.
1879	The first practical light bulb is invented.
1914	World War I begins.
1917	The Bolshevik Revolution brings communism to Russia.
1929	A worldwide economic depression begins.
1939	World War II begins.
1945	World War II ends.
1957	The Vietnam War begins.
1969	Humans land on the Moon.
1975	The Vietnam War ends.
1989	The Berlin Wall is torn down as communism crumbles in Eastern Europe.
1991	The Soviet Union breaks into separate states.
2001	Terrorists attack the World Trade Center in New York City and the Pentagon in Washington, D.C.

Fast Facts

Official name: Islamic Republic of Iran

Capital: Tehran

Official language: Persian

Tehran

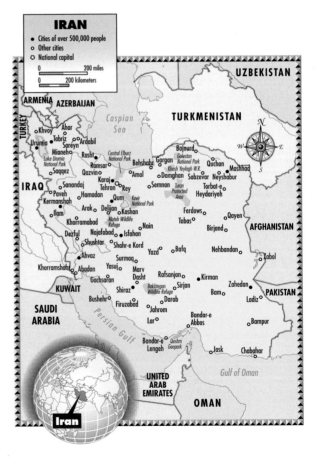

Iran's flag

Tulip

Official religion: Shi'i Islam

Year of founding: 1979

National anthem: "Soroude Jomhuri-e Eslimi-e Iran"
("Anthem of the Islamic Republic of Iran")

Government: Islamic republic

Head of state: Supreme leader

Head of government: President

Area: 635,932 square miles (1,647,064 sq km)

**Greatest distance
north to south:** 810 miles (1,300 km)

**Greatest distance
east to west:** 860 miles (1,375 km)

Land borders: Armenia, Azerbaijan, and Turkmenistan to the
north; Afghanistan and Pakistan to the east; Iraq
and Turkey to the west

Water borders: The Caspian Sea to the north; the Persian Gulf
and the Gulf of Oman to the south

Highest elevation: 18,934 feet (5,771 m) above sea level, at
Mount Damavand

Lowest elevation: 92 feet (28 m) below sea level,
along the Caspian Sea coast

Average temperatures:

	January	July
Tehran	35°F (2°C)	85°F (29°C)
Khuzistan Plain	54°F (12°C)	97°F (36°C)

**Highest average
annual precipitation:** 80 inches (200 cm), in the lowlands along the
Caspian Sea

Hafiz's tomb

Currency

Lowest average annual precipitation:	2 inches (5 cm), in parts of the desert
National population (2006 est.):	69 million

Population of largest cities:

Tehran	14,000,000
Mashhad	2,000,000
Tabriz	1,700,000
Isfahan	1,000,000
Shiraz	850,000

Famous landmarks:
- ▶ *Azadi Tower*, Tehran
- ▶ *Badgirs (wind towers)*, Yazd
- ▶ *Blue Mosque*, Tabriz
- ▶ *Hafiz's tomb*, Shiraz
- ▶ *Imam Square*, Isfahan
- ▶ *Persepolis*

Industry: Oil is the leading industry in Iran by far. The second most important industry is textile manufacture, especially Persian carpets. The country also makes automobiles, cement, processed food, and steel. Major crops include wheat, barley, sugar beets, and sugarcane.

Currency: The rial. In 2007, US$1 equaled more than 9,000 rials.

System of weights and measures: Metric system

Literacy rate: 77%

Internet café

Shirin Ebadi

Common Persian words and phrases:		
	bale	yes
	na	no
	salam	hello
	madar	mother
	pedar	father
	khoda hafez	good-bye
	Haletun chetur e?	How are you?
	motashakkeram	thank you
	Khahesh mikonam.	You are welcome.
	lotfan	please

Famous Iranians:		
	Cyrus the Great *Achaemenid ruler*	(600–529 B.C.)
	Darius I *Achaemenid ruler*	(558–486 B.C.)
	Shirin Ebadi *Winner of the Nobel Peace Prize*	(1947–)
	Hakim Abulqasim Ferdosi *Poet*	(ca. 940–1020)
	Hafiz (Khwaja Shams-ed-Din Muhammad) *Poet*	(1324–1398)
	Omar Khayyam *Poet*	(1047?–1123?)
	Ayatollah Ruhollah Khomeini *Leader of the Islamic Revolution*	(1900–1989)
	Mohsen Makhmalbaf *Filmmaker*	(1957–)

To Find Out More

Books

▶ Gholamrezaei, Shabnam. *Fiesta Iran*. Danbury, CT: Grolier, 2004.

▶ Kalman, Bobbie. *Iran*. New York: Crabtree Publishing, 2005.

▶ Russell, Malcolm B. *The Middle East and South Asia 2006*. World Today Series. Baltimore: Stryker-Post Publications, 2006.

▶ Satrapi, Marjane. *Persepolis: The Story of a Childhood*. New York: Pantheon Graphic Novels, 2003.

▶ Sheen, Barbara. *Foods of Iran*. Farmington Hills, MI: Kidhaven Press, 2006.

DVDs

▶ *Blackboards*. Wellspring Media, 2004. Teachers roam the Iranian countryside in search of students.

▶ *Children of Heaven*. Miramax, 2002. A boy loses his sister's shoes and must share his sneakers with her.

▶ *Ten*. Zeitgeist Films, 2002. A woman driving through Tehran has conversations with ten female passengers and her own young son.

▶ *The White Balloon*. October Films, 1996. A young girl sets out to buy a goldfish, but she loses her money and must retrieve it.

Web Sites

▶ **Iran Chamber Society**
www.iranchamber.com
For information about the art, history, and culture of Iran.

▶ **MehrNews.com**
www.mehrnews.com/en/
To read news about Iran from an Iranian news agency.

▶ **Qoqnoos**
www.qoqnoos.com
For a glimpse of a wide variety of Iranian artists, writers, and musicians.

▶ **The World Factbook: Iran**
www.cia.gov/library/publications/
the-world-factbook/geos/ir.html
For quick facts about Iran's geography, people, and government.

Embassies and Organizations

▶ **Embassy of the Islamic Republic of Iran in Canada**
245 Metcalfe Street
Ottawa, Ontario
K2P 2K2 Canada
613-233-4726
www.salamiran.org/embassy

Index

Page numbers in *italics* indicate illustrations.

Meet the Author

JoAnn Milivojevic is a freelance writer and video producer who loves to travel and explore the world. She lives in Chicago, Illinois, which is home to people from many cultures, including Iran. She had the pleasure of meeting many Iranians in Chicago while doing research for this book and is grateful for their hospitality and enthusiasm. They shared their culture with her and endured her many questions. They also invited her to a Persian New Year's celebration and introduced her to traditional Persian food. She has since cooked Persian meals for her own friends and family.

When writing about a country like Iran, it is all too easy to get caught up in current news and politics. But that is just a small part of a country's story. To research Iran, Milivojevic read many books, newspaper and magazine articles, and Web sites about things Iranian. Through the Internet, she also met Iranian people and saw pictures of places in Iran that she hopes to someday see for herself.

Milivojevic's career as a writer has allowed her to pursue her interest in world cultures. She has written several other

books for the Enchantment of the World series, including *Serbia*, *Bosnia*, and the *Czech Republic*. She has also traveled extensively in the Caribbean while working on writing assignments. Although she loves the sea, sun, and sand, it is meeting people that makes her travels worthwhile.

Milivojevic has a bachelor of arts degree from Indiana University. Before becoming a writer, she worked as a radio and television producer. Today, in addition to her work as a children's book writer, she writes about fitness, food, and travel for magazines and newspapers nationwide. Milivojevic's dog, Tolstoy, is her writing partner. He reminds her every day that roaming the great outdoors is as important to writing as tapping away at the keyboard.

Photo Credits